GUNNER
My Life
in Cricket

GUNNER
My Life
in Cricket

IAN GOULD

First published by Pitch Publishing, 2020

Pitch Publishing
A2 Yeoman Gate
Yeoman Way
Worthing
Sussex
BN13 3QZ
www.pitchpublishing.co.uk
info@pitchpublishing.co.uk

ISBN 978 1 78531 630 2

Typesetting and origination by Pitch Publishing
Printed and bound by TJ International, Padstow, UK

Contents

Picture credits: James Boardman/Telephoto Images (cover); Getty Images; Sussex Cricket Museum; other images are from the author's family archive.

The author would also like to thank Mark Baldwin and Andrea Dunn for checking the text and making helpful suggestions.

Foreword by Jeff Crowe

THIS wonderful game of cricket generously offers so much to its followers. A fiercely fought contest can produce a jaw-dropping spectacle that simply takes your breath away. But for me, that is not what makes cricket so great.

As a past player, team manager and now an administrator the human element has always been the most satisfying for me. Among cricketers a genuine camaraderie exists from which lasting friendships are formed.

Once upon a time in Auckland, at the beautiful Cornwall Cricket Club ground, I walked into the home dressing room one afternoon and there in the corner was Ian James Gould, sitting with a young wicketkeeper called Adam Parore.

Tongue in cheek, Ian quipped: 'Alright guv, all's going well. It's all yours.' He was caretaker skipper while I was on provincial duty. That was close to 40 years ago back in the early 1980s and it was the beginning of an extraordinary cricketing bond.

We had come across each other before when Ian was representing Middlesex and England. He also played for another local club, Ellerslie, as well as Auckland, so I saw a lot of him during the next few Kiwi summers. Ian and his darling wife Jo loved their time in Auckland and the city embraced them big time. They are worldly, warm and engaging. You know, proper people.

After coaching Middlesex, Gunner turned to umpiring and it could be argued this was something that became more important to him than playing for his country.

He became a brilliant umpire and, as luck would have it, we became reacquainted after I joined the ICC's match referee panel. We were to travel the cricketing world again and this time on the same team.

He was undoubtedly the best man-manager I have ever seen among on-field umpires. His ability to read players, engage and be able to control them was extraordinary. Players respected him while TV commentators all over the world regularly remarked on how skilled Gunner was in his decision-making. Even when it got tense in the middle he just knew how to take command of the situation. Erroneously in my opinion, he was never awarded the ICC Umpire of the Year.

My brother Martin was a great fan and mate of Gunner. Martin told me one day that he thought Gunner's technique when raising his finger to give someone out wasn't as English as it might be and suggested he change to raising a pointed finger in front of the eyes pointing towards the batsman instead. While we were in Dominica prior to a Test match I mentioned this to him and we went straight to the nets. Gunner practised for a while with some different styles until we finally agreed on one. I took a photograph of it and sent it back to Martin for his approval. Ian now had a new dismissal delivery technique.

I always enjoyed catching up with Gunner, whether it was in the hustle and bustle of Dhaka or the white sands of a Caribbean beach. There were always places to see and enjoy on non-matchdays with him.

And usually I knew where to find him. Once, on arriving at our hotel in Jolly Beach, Antigua, I walked out on to these gorgeous sands and looked left and right. 'I bet he's at that far end of the beach,' I thought. And there he was, sitting in a Tiki hut with the locals, swilling and chilling.

Just like when we connected in Cape Town prior to the third Test between South Africa and Australia in 2018, the infamous 'Sandpaper Test'. I had completed the first two Tests and the cricket had been as acrimonious as any. 'Don't worry, we'll sort it from now on my son,' he said. And he did.

Ian's contribution to cricket has been enormous. He is rightly respected as a player, coach and latterly an international elite match official. It was an honour and delight making a presentation to Ian before his 100th one-day international in Sydney during the 2015 World Cup.

As he did at Cornwall Park for me way back, during these last years I was always nearby and willing to be his caretaker when needed.

People love his classic cockney style, sharp dry wit and his ever-present broad smile. Gunner never wants much fuss and he will always try to uphold the standards and traditions of the game.

When we disagreed on anything he always starts: 'I've known you for a very long time … !'

Ian's story in cricket is unique. County player, county captain, England player, county coach and world-class umpire. He has an incredible amount to share and to tell from both on and off the field and through these absorbing chapters all will be revealed.

'Salut' and go well my son, it will continue to be an absolute pleasure.

And it's your round!

Jeff (Chopper) Crowe

Jeff Crowe played more than 100 times for New Zealand including 39 Tests before spending four years as manager of the team. He has been an ICC match referee since 2004.

Acknowledgements

CRICKET has given me a fantastic life and I have met some wonderful people but two people in particular have played a big part in my story so far. When I was growing up in Cippenham, my PE teacher Terry Davies guided me in the right way. Thank you, Terry.

I would not have enjoyed the career I did in umpiring without the support, time and guidance so generously given by my coach Denis Burns.

When I first had the idea to tell my story shortly before my retirement from the ICC elite panel in 2019, I didn't have much idea about what it involved. It has amazed me that a year later you are reading a book of which I am extremely proud.

Peter Jacob is a cricket writer I have known for more than 30 years. Over many sessions in a couple of my favourite Hove hostelries (drinking coffee only before you ask!) he helped put my thoughts and stories on to paper. Similarly, my grateful thanks to everyone at Pitch Publishing for their support.

Sadly, my father George, mother Doreen, sister Maureen and brother Barrie are not here to read it. May *Gunner – My Life in Cricket* be a loving remembrance to them.

Finally, I could not have done this without the love and support of my wife Jo, who has given me the time, space and freedom to work on my book. My incredible children Gemma, Michael and George, brother Jeff and beautiful grandchildren Ava, Mya and Neo are a wonderful team to have around me.

Ian Gould, Hove, March 2020

1

Line in the Sand

I KNOW this might surprise a few people who love cricket and watch a lot of it, but most top umpires prepare for games as fastidiously as players. From the day I joined the International Cricket Council (ICC)'s elite panel in 2008, two years after I stood in my first international at the Oval, I trained for every game, and in particular Test matches, in pretty much the same way and certainly with a bit more professionalism than when I played for England back in the 1980s when warm-ups usually consisted of a few laps of the outfield and some stretches with the physio Bernard Thomas, who was the equivalent of a modern-day strength and conditioning coach back then.

Two days before the game started, I would go down to the ground, dump my gear in the umpires' room, wander over to the nets and stand at one end during each team's practice and just observe. When you think about it, it's an obvious thing to do. The international game moves so quickly these days that when I began a new series in a different country there were invariably bowlers and batsmen who I had not come across before. So, I stood there quietly, getting used to the pace and bounce of the wicket – which is quite often pretty consistent with the pitch they are going to use for the match – and just see what's going on. As everyone in cricket knows, I'm a pretty gregarious person so it was also a nice opportunity to say hello to players I've umpired before, meet new ones and get some feedback on them from the coaches before chewing the fat with the groundsman or the dozens of administrators and media people that are invariably milling around any ground in the days before every international fixture.

But most importantly, it's a time when I could prepare mentally and physically for what's coming: things like adjusting your eyes to the light, which varies so much from country to country or sometimes even ground to ground, getting accustomed to any changes in the background like new stands that you've not seen before or working out where the nearest toilet is if you get caught short during a long session of play – which happens quite a lot, I can tell you. A couple of hours sharpens you up and gets you back into focus. I can't say that my method of preparation is followed by all of the other leading umpires. In fact, I think it's a bit of a dying art. But each to their own, as long as they can do the job.

The day before the third Test between South Africa and Australia at Newlands in Cape Town in March 2018 – which was to be the 89th of my career if you count third-umpire duties, or 64th if you don't – was no different, at least in terms of my own preparation. Myself and my English colleagues Richard Illingworth and Nigel Llong had been appointed for the second half of the series, which also involved a fourth Test match in Johannesburg. Richard flew down from Manchester and we all got the overnight flight from Heathrow to Cape Town. Generally, umpires from the same country try to travel together. I've always had a brilliant relationship with those two gentlemen and when you're catching up it doesn't half make a ten-hour flight go quicker. That and a couple of beers, of course.

I don't remember watching much of either of the first two Tests. I love cricket but I get bored quickly if I'm sitting at home in front of the TV looking at it. If it is a choice between a Test match or a decent jumps card at Fontwell or Newton Abbot on the racing channel, it would be the horses every time. But I was very aware that there had been no love lost between South Africa and Australia in the first two Tests. A few days before I headed to Cape Town, Chris Gaffaney, the very capable New Zealander who was third umpire for the first Test in Durban and had stood with Kumar Dharmasena in Port Elizabeth in the second match, left a message on my phone, warning me that things were starting to get a little bit out of hand. The umpiring team had their suspicions that Australia were working a little too aggressively on the condition of the ball, and they had an informal word with the host broadcaster SuperSport asking that if their camera crew saw anything that looked unusual they should let the umpires know.

Chris wasn't wrong when he claimed things were getting out of hand. It had started on the second day of the first Test when the Australian players tried to get the stump microphones turned down by shouting the names of rival companies to those that were sponsoring the series. A couple of days later Nathan Lyon was fined 15 per cent of his match fee for dropping the ball on AB de Villiers after running him out and then David Warner and Quinton de Kock argued heatedly as they left the field and were also disciplined. A couple of days after that Tim Paine, the Australia wicketkeeper, denied that they had personally abused de Kock while he was batting. 'We didn't cross the line,' he insisted.

With the first two Tests back to back, there wasn't much time for things to calm down. On the first day in Port Elizabeth, Kagiso Rabada, the South Africa fast bowler who I was encountering for the first time in that series, brushed shoulders with Steve Smith when he got him out before giving Warner an earful of abuse. Having come into the series with four demerit points to his name, Rabada was subsequently banned for two matches, but there was no way South Africa were going to take that lying down, especially with a series as important as this on the line and Rabada bowling well. They hired seven lawyers, including David Becker, the former head of ICC's legal department, and persuaded the authorities that Rabada hadn't made contact with Smith deliberately. It must have cost them a few thousand rand in legal fees, but it worked. His punishment was reduced to one demerit point which meant he was free to play in the third Test.

To add fuel to the fire, Mitchell Marsh was fined for swearing at Rabada after getting him out. South Africa won the match though, so the series was level at 1-1 as they headed to Cape Town. And while all this was going on, Warner – who was in charge of looking after the condition of the ball for Australia – was taking to the field with the fingers of his left hand strapped up. He even wrote the name of his wife and his kids on the bandages when he realised how much scrutiny his hand was under from the TV cameras.

When I stood in the Cape Town nets and Rabada came steaming past me for the first time I was very impressed. He had a fantastic action, got good bounce and was very quick – even in practice he made a couple of his team-mates hop around a bit. He seemed a really nice man too. We had a little chat. He told me he was going to keep his temper under control, but the vibes that day weren't great. I'd been umpiring at the top level for 12 years by then and after just an hour or so I could sense it might get a bit lively again.

The South Africans had been intrigued as to how Mitchell Starc, Australia's very skilful left-arm fast bowler, had been able to swing it so much in Durban and Port Elizabeth, two venues where the Kookaburra ball didn't do a great deal off the straight. In my experience Starc can make it hoop around without doing anything naughty, and I told a couple of the South African players this during that net session. That issue seemed to have been put to bed but the Aussies were still steaming that Rabada had not been banned.

Anyway, I was standing there minding my own business when David Warner came up to me. We shook hands. I've umpired Davey many times and he's a nice bloke, but he is very competitive on the field and always has been. He likes to have a word or two. After the pleasantries, he said to me: 'Well Gunner, where's the fucking line in the sand now?' And that was it – he walked off and left me with those words hanging in the air. Here we go, I thought.

In hindsight, ICC's decision not to bring Illy, Nige and myself in until the third Test was a mistake. Two of the three lads who did the first two Tests were relatively inexperienced. Dharmasena had stood in over 50 Tests but Chris was in only his 19th game and the other umpire, Sundaram Ravi from India, had fewer than 25 Tests under his belt and within a year or so had been kicked off the elite panel because he wasn't deemed good enough.

Look, they were by no means poor at their job, but someone in the ICC hierarchy ought to have looked at that series, which Australia came into on the back of thumping England in the Ashes and were looking to become world number one, and decided it needed a team of their most experienced men. South Africa on home soil were never going to lie down and have their backsides kicked and, in Rabada, they obviously had a relatively unknown quantity who was prepared to give the Aussie quicks as good as they got. Like I said, hindsight is a wonderful thing but I'm absolutely sure the English trio including me would have got on top of things from the off. More things had happened in those first two Tests than you normally have to deal with in a five-match series.

Fortunately, what we did have in Cape Town and for the fourth Test in Johannesburg was a top match referee in Andy Pycroft, who had taken over from another good man in Jeff Crowe. As it turned out, Andy, who is a lawyer when he's not sitting in cricket grounds, was the perfect appointment. Andy had played at the highest level for Zimbabwe and knew the game and what went on inside out. With Andy, the paperwork was always spot on and we ended up having to do a lot of form-filling during those few days. But first, we met with the captains and coaches on the afternoon before the Test, warned them about their responsibilities and wished them luck. Everything seemed to be fine. We were good to go.

And for the first two days there was absolutely no hint that this Test would go down in history for all the wrong reasons. While Illy and Nige were out in the middle, I sat in the third umpires' room with Andy, minding my own business. One of the third umpire's more mundane duties is to keep a count to make sure six balls are bowled in each over – you'd be amazed the number of times umpires can't count to six (myself included) – so you have to stay awake and concentrate, but third-umpire stints are pretty uneventful most of the time. You want to be out there, not forever checking this and that on a TV screen. By mid-afternoon you're already thinking about what restaurant to book for the evening.

Dean Elgar carried his bat in South Africa's first-innings score of 311 and Pat Cummins took four wickets before Australia struggled a little in reply, making 255. Cameron Bancroft scored 70 and Rabada took another four wickets but by the third day the Newlands pitch had really flattened out as it tended to do. It was a typically dry, baking-hot Cape Town afternoon as South Africa set about batting Australia out of the game in their second innings.

Early in the afternoon, all hell broke loose. The SuperSport TV director Eddie came through on my earpiece. 'Gunner, we've got something that you and the on-field umpires need to look at.' Andy was doing some paperwork and I tapped him on the shoulder. Then we saw the first pictures on our monitor of Cameron Bancroft, who was fielding in the covers, applying something which had a yellow side to it on to the ball. The TV director came back on to confirm he was going to show this incident at the end of the next over, so I contacted Illy and Llongy straightaway on the walkie-talkie, during the middle of the over.

Although this was a serious incident that would have dramatic repercussions for Australian cricket it was also very funny because of a couple of incidents that only the players and umpires knew about at the time. Andy Pycroft saw the footage first and said 'Shit.' I was thinking to myself, 'How do I handle this without creating a drama and exacerbating the situation? I have to deal with this. No simulation or preparation has covered this one.' Our coaches run through TV umpire simulations with the guys, but

I've never been a big fan. I prefer to think on my feet rather than go through hypotheticals in a Skype call. My coach Denis Burns had suspected that I'd wiped the Skype app off my laptop a long time ago:

Denis: 'Can we have a simulation on Skype?'

'On what?'

Denis: 'On Skype; it was installed on your laptop by our IT technicians.'

'Hang on. We've got BBC, Virgin, and Netflix. What channel is it on?'

'Oh dear!'

Mission accomplished. Denis knew I wasn't interested. Illy came back on: 'What now, in the middle of an over?'

I didn't want to spook them and cause a drama, so I said: 'Boys, take a deep breath, stay calm and come together away from the players.' I then explained what I had seen, and they prepared themselves to talk to the players.

The boys wandered over to him, and captain Steve Smith joined them a few moments later. Cameron Bancroft produced a black cloth, the sort the players use to clean their sunglasses. The on-field umpires relayed this information to me and Andy, and the game carried on. No need to change the ball or anything – back to the cricket. From an umpiring perspective, it went well. No histrionics, no dramas, just a discussion. Both umpires spoke to Denis that evening and told him that my calm attitude had worked and that they were relaxed and composed when talking to the players. I was proud of that. All the time, what later emerged to be sandpaper was hiding down Bancroft's trousers and the cameras had filmed him putting it there.

While all this drama was unfolding around us, Andy Pycroft took a phone call from David Richardson, the chief executive of ICC, and gave me a message to relay to the umpires. I laughed. 'You can't be serious!' Here we go again.

'Boys, take a deep breath, stay calm and come together away from the players.'

'Oh no, what's happened now? Not the same again?'

'No, I've just had a phone call from the ICC.'

'Nice one, do they want to congratulate us on the way we've handled everything?'

'Not quite. Stay calm, and ask Nathan Lyon what colour socks he's wearing?'

[Laughter] 'Seriously? Go on, what's the punchline?'

'No punchline, seriously. They think that Nathan is wearing black socks. Ask him to show you his socks.'

'They want us to ask Nathan Lyon what colour socks he's wearing, in the middle of this shitstorm?'

'Please.'

They called Nathan over.

'Nathan, Gunner would like to know what colour socks you are wearing.'

'What the ****. Are you ******* kidding me? That takes the ******* biscuit. Tell Gunner he can **** off.'

'Now, now my son. Please put some white socks on. Standards please!'

'******! Okay, ******.'

'Thank you.'

Seriously, you could not make it up. We were trying to keep the lid on a volatile international incident and someone, somewhere in the world, had noticed the bowler was wearing the wrong colour of socks. Nathan came back on to the field and yanked his trousers up so that the umpires could see his pristine white socks. All in a day's work.

At tea, the three of us and Andy sat in the room discussing what had happened. By now the story was really starting to gather some momentum, especially on social media. We decided to bring together Bancroft, Steve Smith and Gavin Dovey, the Australia team manager, for a chat after play. If Bancroft was ball-tampering, he would be banned for one match. The evidence against him, it's fair to say, was starting to stack up. Thankfully, it's the job of the match referee to do the form-filling and Andy spent most of the final session getting that right. After play, we chatted again and were happy we had got our processes right. Throughout all of this I had been amazingly composed. In fact, the others were surprised at how measured I'd been. It was all down to experience, I suppose.

I didn't watch the post-match press conference involving Smith and Bancroft where they confessed to using sandpaper on the ball but there were enough people around Newlands that evening who could tell me what had happened. We were still at the ground, packing up to go back to the hotel, when there was a knock on the door. In walked Cameron Bancroft looking absolutely terrible. We had realised from very early in proceedings that he wasn't the brains behind the operation, or part of this so-called leadership group in the Australian camp which we were now becoming aware of.

I guess, desperate to do the right thing as a newish player trying to establish himself in the team, he'd stuck his hand up to look after the ball instead of David Warner. We offered him a beer, which he declined although he looked as if he could have done with several. 'Look guys, I'm here to apologise for lying to you today,' he said. 'It's not in my character and I'm not that sort of person. I am really, really sorry.'

To be fair, I thought it was a very brave thing to do. He'd slipped out of the dressing rooms unnoticed to come and speak to us in person, without consulting Steve Smith, Gavin Dovey or anyone else in the Australia camp. He probably felt a bit better afterwards but neither he nor us could imagine the shitstorm that was coming when Australians woke up back home the next morning to the news that their cricketers had been caught cheating red-handed.

The Cullinan Hotel in Cape Town was the place to be for the next few days, not Newlands where the game itself completely lost its intensity. The great and the good of Australian cricket flew in to handle the aftermath of 'Sandpaper-gate'. Within hours the Australian prime minister Malcolm Turnbull was leading the criticism back home, and a few days later

Smith and Warner – captain and vice-captain – had copped year-long bans and Bancroft nine months. Smith and Warner made tearful returns home, a long-overdue review into the culture at the top of their game was underway and Australian cricket had changed forever. Before the fourth Test at Johannesburg, Darren Lehmann had resigned as coach as well.

I struggled to keep up with events, which were moving so fast. As umpires all we could do was satisfy ourselves that we'd done our jobs properly during that incident. There was certainly nothing said by either team or the ICC to the contrary against us. But what a mess, and what an embarrassment for the game itself.

Meanwhile, a Test match and a series still had to be finished. Tim Paine, a really nice guy who almost gave up the game before forcing his way back into the Australia team, took over from Smith but there was little he could do to prevent South Africa from hammering them in Cape Town. They won by 322 runs to go 2-1 up in the series and when we all reconvened in Johannesburg a few days later we knew it wouldn't be too long before they would win the series 3-1.

That Test was the weirdest I had ever been involved in. It was like umpiring a schools' match.

Every decision we made was accepted without challenge and it was hilariously quiet. No one sledged and to be honest it was really hard work concentrating – there was nothing to get your teeth into. After what had happened in the first three Tests you might have thought we'd have all been grateful for a bit of peace and quiet, but most umpires are no different to players – we like a bit of an edge to proceedings. Most of the Australian players were walking around like zombies. Lehmann had resigned on the eve of the Test and although Paine did his best and said all the right things about it being the start of a new era for his team – the sides even agreed to shake hands before the game started to show there were no hard feelings – the bitterness and resentment Australia felt was never too far below the surface.

I'm quite a nervous umpire. I've always tried to have absolute clarity when I make my decisions, but we can feel the pressure as much as the players do on occasion. For me, this manifests itself occasionally in a really dry mouth. So I always have a few sweets – normally Werther's Originals – in my pocket to get me through the day, whether I'm umpiring in Hove or Hobart. It's part of my routine and so it was at the Wanderers during that fourth Test. At the end of day one I was walking off, put my hand in my pocket and one of the wrappers fell out. I pushed it down a stump hole with my boot on one of the pitches on the edge of the square and thought nothing more of it.

The following morning the Australian bowlers were doing their warm-ups on the same wicket. You can probably guess what happened next. A few minutes later their bowling coach David Saker knocked on our door and came in. 'We've got 'em!' he said. By that, we took it to mean that my sweet wrapper he had in his hand was the evidence that the South Africans had been applying saliva from Werther's Originals to get the ball to swing on what was another flat deck.

I looked at Andy and he looked at me, and both of us tried to keep a straight face. I reached into my pocket and rolled a couple of Werther's along the table towards Saker. 'These sweets you mean?' How Andy stopped himself dissolving into fits of laughter I'll never know. It was a ridiculous accusation to make on the flimsiest of evidence but that's how bad things had got between the teams. They were paranoid.

Nathan Lyon tried to wind up a few of the South Africans in Johannesburg with some verbals, and even after I had spoken to the Australian management to tell him to shut up it continued. Nothing over the top, but it seemed Nathan wasn't yet on board with the brave new world of Australian cricket. I had a chat with Allan Border, who was commentating on the series for TV and had been disgusted that his country's cricketing reputation had been dragged into the gutter. By all accounts, and with the full knowledge of their chairman of selectors Trevor Hohns, Border gave Lyon an old-fashioned bollocking and, to his credit, Nathan then apologised to me and the other umpires and we had another laugh about his socks.

South Africa won the game easily. Aiden Markram and Faf du Plessis made hundreds and when South Africa declared at tea on day four, setting Australia more than 600 to win, I just wanted them to be put out of their misery quickly. On the final day Vernon Philander took six wickets, but South Africa's celebrations at the end were fairly muted. It had been a horrible couple of weeks and I was glad to be heading home but not until I'd made sure I had some important items in my baggage.

After Cape Town I'd collected the match balls that had been used and put them in a box. I contacted the ICC's anti-corruption unit and reported that I was taking them for safekeeping. I didn't want them being mistaken for practice balls, which would in all likelihood have been scuffed and marked, and then picked out, potentially identified as the ball we'd played with in the game and possibly used to implicate a player or players. Steve was happy so I brought them back to England. They are in a vault in a bank in London where I keep all my personal stuff. No one has ever asked for them and there isn't a mark on any of them, apart from our signatures for verification. I wonder if anyone will ever ask for them back?

2

I'm Out

IT was back in 2014 when ICC first mooted to us that the retirement age for an umpire on the elite panel would be 62. The first of my colleagues to fall victim to this decree was Tony Hill, a lovely guy from New Zealand who had joined the elite panel at the same time as me in 2009. Tony umpired his last Test in 2015 a few weeks after he turned 62 and then Steve Davis stepped down later that year a few weeks after he turned 63. Both were terrific umpires with lots of experience but when you've got to go, you've got to go.

The problem I had with this was nothing was said, or communicated officially in writing or email, by ICC to inform you that you stopped at 62 and, to my knowledge, there still hasn't been. The irony of my departure in June 2019, during the World Cup in England, is that it came when I felt I was umpiring better than at any time in my career. I'd go as far to say that over the three years before I retired from the international circuit, I had actually improved my level of skill. Even when I was occasionally struggling to concentrate, I went back to using an old trick whereby I actually commentated on the game. Now, obviously I wouldn't say, 'It's Glenn McGrath coming in from the Paddington End bowling to Sachin Tendulkar ...' Rather, I used the two players who were facing each other when I stood in a first-class match for the first time back in 2001. Durham v Durham University. 'And it's Neil Killeen coming in to bowl to Michael Brown ...' One international bowler stopped in his run-up when he heard that, but it has always helped me stay focused.

I felt much more relaxed. I'd had some serious mental health issues in 2015-16, which you will read about later, but I was loving my job again. During the next three years or so, I reckon I got around 97–98 per cent of my decisions right – not bad in an era when the Decision Review System (DRS) started to become prevalent and put umpires under much more pressure. But with me there was always that little doubt in the back of my mind that perhaps things were going too well. And it did start to nag away that the year-long ICC contract I renewed in June 2018 might be my last. I was 61 at the time.

But if I had to go at 62, I was determined it was going to be on my terms. No one was going to drag me kicking and screaming from a cricket ground, against my will or otherwise. In November 2018 I was appointed to umpire two Tests in Abu Dhabi between Pakistan and New Zealand and when I saw that two of my favourite colleagues, Bruce Oxenford of New Zealand and Paul Reiffel from Australia, would be there with me I decided to tell them that I was packing it in, come what may. I could trust them not to tell a soul until it became official. Did I want them to urge me to reconsider? Maybe a little part of me wanted the reassurance from two guys I really admired that yes, I was making the right decision. And maybe a little part of me wanted them to boost my ego a bit by telling me that if I could I should carry on. After all, where was it in writing that I had to quit at 62?

I knew I was good enough to continue and, although I had long since stopped reading the report on my performances compiled by the match referee, the marks I got in the previous two years or so from the captains of the series which I umpired confirmed that. Throughout my decade or so on the elite panel, I was probably what you might call our shop steward in discussions with ICC. Not quite Arthur Scargill but I was always the one who asked the awkward questions, even if on occasion it got me into trouble. It's a small regret of mine that I didn't at least get written confirmation put into our contracts that said 62 was when you'd have to pack up. It could have saved me a lot of inner turmoil.

In the end, as with most of the major decisions in my life, family held sway. Before heading to Abu Dhabi I talked it over with my wife Jo and our three kids, Gemma, who works in local government in Berkshire, Michael, who sells cricket equipment for Newbery at the County Ground in Hove, and George, who runs the groundsmanship business I set up over 20 years ago. They told me that if I wanted to retire then I just had to get on and do it. 'Don't worry about us,' said Michael. But they did warn me about changing my mind or being talked out of it by ICC. I've got three lovely grandchildren and what the kids didn't want was me telling them I'd be around a bit more and then have to say a few months later that, actually, grandad is off on his travels again for ten weeks. A bit of emotional blackmail perhaps, but it worked.

I don't know why I got myself up into a bit of a lather about my decision, but I definitely felt the need to unburden myself when Bruce Oxenford, Paul Reiffel and I met up for a drink a few days before the first Pakistan–New Zealand Test in Abu Dhabi. I don't think they were that surprised. They both knew as well that 62 was the magic number. Even then, I stalled on telling anyone at ICC about my decision. We decided to reconvene after the series finished when I was due to stand with Paul, having done the first match with Bruce. I just wanted to be absolutely sure.

And I had another really good series. The first Test was an absolute classic which New Zealand won by four runs after Ajaz Patel, their debutant off-spinner, took five wickets. Pakistan won the second game easily by an innings to set up a series finale which was dominated by Kane Williamson, who made 89 and 139 to help New Zealand win by 123 runs. Jo had flown out to join me for the final Test and afterwards we all met up again. There was no going back. 'I'm out,' I told them. I shook hands with Bruce and Paul at the airport and, as usual, we vowed to toast each other's health with a glass of champagne at 38,000 feet as we made our way home.

A few weeks later I was driving to Heathrow again, this time to fly to Australia to do their series against India including the Boxing Day Test in Melbourne and the Sydney Test at New Year. I'd still heard nothing from ICC about my future. As far as I was concerned it was business as usual. But looking back a year or so later, I do wish that the Sydney match had been my final Test. In Melbourne I stood with the South African Marais Erasmus, one of the most charming and loveable blokes I have ever met, and then in Sydney with England's Richard Kettleborough, who is an outstanding umpire and a brilliant guy as well. This was Australia's first major series since the Cape Town affair and with a new coach (Justin Langer) and new captain (Tim Paine) they behaved like choirboys. India won the series 2-1 but that margin flattered the Aussies. In Sydney, India ran up 600 before it rained for virtually the rest of the match.

It was the third time I had stood in a Boxing Day Test at the Melbourne Cricket Ground and once again it was a fantastic occasion. The first-day crowd was 73,516 and I absolutely revelled in it. I was standing with one of my favourite colleagues, the place was absolutely heaving, and I had a bird's-eye view of some of the best cricketers in the world. Wow. This was the players' stage of course but I was playing a small part and that still felt like an amazing privilege for me. For a few moments, when I walked out there on day one in front of that huge crowd and that sense of anticipation that only the first morning of a Test match can bring, I did wonder if I should dig my heels in and make an argument for carrying on beyond 62. But that feeling disappeared by the time I got to the middle. There was no going back. My mind was made up.

After a few weeks off at the start of 2019 I was away again, this time to South Africa for their series against Sri Lanka. Alongside me were Aleem Dar and Richard Kettleborough. I'd still had nothing in writing from ICC and, when I walked off the field at Port Elizabeth on 25 February, I still wasn't sure that I had just completed my 74th and final Test (99 if you include third-umpire duties). It was, in fairness, a wonderful series. South Africa were supposed to roll them over, but Sri Lanka squeezed home by one wicket in Durban and then completed an astonishing 2-0 series win by eight wickets in the second Test. It wasn't a series that set the pulses racing among the home fans. The second match only lasted three days and when Sri Lanka completed an easy victory the crowd was no bigger than you'd get for a County Championship game at home. In hindsight, I should perhaps have forced the issue earlier with ICC, but I still hadn't told them my plans to retire. Signing off from Test cricket in Sydney or Melbourne would have been infinitely more satisfying than in front of one man and his dog in Port Elizabeth.

Finally, when I got home in March 2019, I found the gumption to let ICC know my thoughts. Now, I'm not very good at expressing myself in emails or letters. I much prefer face-to-face communication, but I was buggered if I was going to fly to their headquarters in Dubai just to hand in my notice. Instead, I spoke to my coach Denis Burns, who'd worked with me since 2013 when he was appointed by ICC. Denis is a former university lecturer and a very clever guy, as well as being an absolute gent.

Instead of writing to the high-ups at ICC, the email was sent to the four members of the Elite Umpires Appointments Panel: David Boon, Sanjay Manjrekar, Geoff Allardice and Ranjan Madugalle.

This is what we put together in April 2019, although the words were written by Denis.

To the ICC Selection Panel
Ranjan Madugalle, Sanjay Manjrekar, David
Boon, Geoff Allardice
On behalf of Ian Gould

Dear Panel,

I have been asked to write this letter on behalf of Ian.

Over the past year Ian has discussed his future as an ICC Elite Umpire in depth with his wife, Jo, his family, and with me, his coach. This letter is written on his behalf and contains his thoughts and wishes, as well as some observations from me in my role as Ian's coach.

'The ultimate measure of a man is not where he stands in moments of comfort and convenience, but where he stands at times of challenge and controversy.'

Martin Luther King Junior

Ian has served the game of cricket with distinction for ten years as an Elite Umpire. His name is synonymous with integrity and Elite Umpiring of the highest order. At times of challenge and controversy he has always, consistently and unflinchingly, done what the game has expected. He has personified the ICC PCT Code of Behaviours and he has been a role model and a source of wisdom for a generation of umpires.

International players and captains recognise his expertise and mastery of man- and game-management and they know the game is safe in his hands. International Panel Umpires acknowledge the powerful, formative influence of working alongside 'Gunner'. He has never hesitated to give his time and formidable energy to further their development.

'I set great store in certain qualities which I believe to be essential in addition to skill. They are that the person conducts his or her life with dignity, with integrity, courage, and perhaps most of all, with modesty.'

Sir Don Bradman

The CWC19 will mark the end of Ian's career with the ICC, he does not wish to be considered for selection at the end of his present contract. With his family he has decided that it is now time to bring this phase of his career in cricket to an end. He has, modestly, requested no ceremonies or fuss to mark his retirement from international umpiring. He also wishes to acknowledge the supportive role of the ICC, and ECB, in appointing him and allowing him to serve the game for so long. He will now devote his energies to preparing for the CWC19 and give the tournament his full, expert commitment to ensure that this showcase of cricket is a great success.

It has been an honour and a privilege to work with one of the great servants of the game,

Denis Burns ICC Umpire Coach

21st April 2019

Sanjay got back in touch straightaway. He was gobsmacked. So too were Boony and Geoff. All three asked me if I was absolutely sure. Madugalle, I heard nothing from, although that wasn't a surprise as we'd had a few run-ins over the years. It was then that I realised that if I'd had a change of mind I could probably have carried on because their opinions carried a lot of sway and if they had recommended that I should continue beyond 62 I would have been able to do so. But I still didn't have any doubts. I wasn't going to miss the travelling and I certainly wasn't going to miss being spat on at airports, which had happened to me a couple of times in India after I made a decision or two which didn't go down well with the local fans.

A couple of weeks later I finally got confirmation from ICC that the World Cup in England would be my international swansong. At last. All I needed to do now was make sure it didn't turn into the 'Gunner Gould Says Goodbye' show. When the news got out I knew there would almost be an expectation that, as the senior man on the panel, I would finish my international career with the Lord's final, providing England didn't get there of course. And if they did, the least I'd get was a semi-final. I soon nipped that in the bud. Before the tournament began the umpires got together for a meeting in London. I deliberately stood next to ICC's Umpires Administrator Adrian Griffith and told him straight. 'I do not under any circumstances want to do a semi-final or the final even if England aren't in it.'

I think he was a bit taken aback but I didn't want emotion to form any part of their decision-making. I had to look my 11 colleagues in the eye remember, all of whom were desperate to be appointed for the semis and final. My imminent departure was not a justification for giving me a big game to finish with. If that was the criteria, I reckon Sundaram Ravi would have got the final. Instead they sacked him a few weeks later because his marks weren't very good.

I know a lot of people inside the game were surprised and a lot of my mates back in Sussex were too that I wouldn't be finishing with a big game. I was just happy to wind down with some lively group matches. I did Australia v India at the Oval, which was a spectacular day, and three games involving New Zealand who are always a pleasure to umpire. Obviously, I wasn't going to be able to stand in an England game but I was happy to bow out with India versus Sri Lanka at a packed Headingley on Saturday 6 July, 44 days before my 62nd birthday.

I'd told ICC in advance that I didn't want any fuss. No interviews, no retirement party, but my plea fell on deaf ears and, once the day was done, I was actually glad that they had ignored me. Kumar Sangakkara and Michael Clarke both paid a nice tribute to me in a film that was shown on TV (which, incidentally, I still haven't seen) and, unbeknown to me until a couple of days before, when my daughter Gemma blurted it out, ICC had organised for Jo and our children to attend the game as their guests in one of the corporate hospitality boxes. They eventually arrived the night before – about two hours after I'd booked a restaurant for us which was typical Gould family timing – and on the morning of the game it was brilliant to be joined by some of my former colleagues, including Bruce Oxenford, Paul Reiffel, Chris Gaffaney and David Boon.

When I walked out to have a look at the wicket before the start, Sanjay Manjrekar, who was working for TV, was still trying to talk me out of retirement. 'Too late,' I said. Sanjay wasn't aware, I think, that another excellent young English umpire, Michael Gough, had already been appointed as my replacement. There really was no going back now. I wish the game itself had been a bit more exciting, but India strolled to victory, winning by seven wickets with 39 balls to spare. It was all over by 6pm. As I was walking off both sets of players shook my hand and Virat Kohli gave me a hug and said some very nice things, which meant a lot.

Sitting in the umpires' room afterwards, with a few of my now former colleagues, reminiscing about the past was the only time that I felt emotional. It was one of the rare occasions when I shed a few tears, apart from at family funerals and when I discovered how much I was being paid after I had joined the elite panel! I managed to hold it together before ICC presented me with a nice montage of sketches from my career. I still haven't hung it up at my home in Hove.

The one the kids had put together with photographs of my career is much better.

Within an hour or so of the game finishing I'd rounded up the family, some of whom had taken full advantage of ICC's generous hospitality, and we were heading back down to Windsor. On the Sunday I'd arranged a 60th birthday party in a pub for Jo which was a wonderful celebration. Life goes on.

I don't hold grudges. Does it rankle that ICC didn't make more of an effort to keep me? Not really. But I would absolutely contend that at 62 the best umpires aren't necessarily past their best. I know I could still do the job. The advent of DRS has put umpires under more scrutiny and pressure than when I started. Will any of the lads have 13 years at the top like me? Somehow, I doubt it. After six or seven years I think most of the guys will have had enough and who can blame them? Look, it's a wonderful career. The chance of watching the best players in the world close up is something I could never get bored of, though they might have had enough of me. I knew I would miss it but it was enough to know that, as I drove out of Leeds that July evening, I was at peace with myself.

3

Teamwork

IN the end I did 13 years as an international umpire before my unexpected 'comeback' at the Under-19 World Cup early in 2020, of which more later. Not bad really. Not many players enjoy a career of that length at the top level. And for the most part I absolutely loved it, although there's no doubt that it became a lot more difficult when Hawkeye and DRS was introduced back in 2011. I remember when Paul Hawkins, who invented the technology, came over to the West Indies in June of that year, when I was umpiring in a Test series against India, to show us how it would operate. Most of us felt the same as Premier League referees in 2019 when the Video Assistant Referee (VAR) was brought in. I was pretty hostile about its introduction and still am.

Now that umpires are doing their jobs under the all-seeing eye of DRS, the pressure on them is much greater than it was when I did my first international in 2006. What I quickly learned was that in a game where DRS was in use you had to leave your ego in the dressing room because you knew that, no matter how good you thought your decision-making was, you could make a mistake that would be picked up by the technology. You had to accept that you might be proved wrong. Or even proved right. It made the job a lot tougher in the second half of my umpiring career.

When I played and when I started umpiring, left-arm round wasn't getting a right-hander out for love nor money, but now DRS was telling us that it could. And it wasn't mandatory back when as to when it was brought in. In 2011 ICC told us they were confident it would soon be in place across the cricket world, but India initially refused to use it. So you would go from a series in, say, Sri Lanka where there were ten cameras and no DRS, to one in Australia where it was in use and there might be 25 or more cameras, and then on to India where it wasn't used at all. So, you could effectively give a batsman out in one match who wasn't out in another. If I made a mistake, I didn't want to be told over the walkie-talkie by the third umpire. Anyway, there was usually a massive replay screen in the ground to put you right. Or a chirpy 12th man who would come on with the drinks and say just loudly enough so all the other players could hear 'you got that one wrong, Gunner'.

How much simpler things were back on 20 June, 2006 when I walked down the steps at the Oval with Darrell Hair to umpire my first one-day international between England and Sri Lanka. I had only been on the English first-class umpires list since 2001 and in those formative years I was lucky because my colleagues included a lot of experienced guys like Peter Willey, Mervyn Kitchen, David Shepherd, Alan Whitehead and David Constant who were great to learn from. They had all played the game and were brilliant at their jobs. I used to soak up their stories like a sponge. I think they recognised that I had a talent and certainly a real enthusiasm for the job and for self-improvement as well as a connection with the players, but also that I needed a few rough edges smoothing down.

I felt the same if the truth be told. As well as playing, I'd also coached a county, so I knew a lot of players. There were still guys on the county circuit whom I'd played against as well as the many I had nurtured at Middlesex, including Andrew Strauss. To go from giving these guys throw-downs in the nets to standing 22 yards away and giving them out in an international match was initially quite a difficult transition for me to make. English county cricket is quite a closed shop really. The players and coaches know each other so well because they play each other so often and so do the umpires. And in those days the reporters who covered their counties or who watched matches for the national papers weren't shy in buying umpires a pint or two after play and getting their cards marked on certain players or things that had happened which they could store away in their notebooks and use further down the line. In short, everyone knew everyone and if you weren't good at your job it would soon be common knowledge.

I still wanted to have a bit of fun, but I quickly learned that I couldn't umpire as an individual, whether it was a Test match or a second XI game in front of a handful of spectators. I had to work as a team with my colleague and have total confidence and trust in him. If you had that, then not a lot would go wrong that you couldn't sort out. I did want to umpire a bit differently, but I soon learned there was a time and a place for a laugh or for getting too involved. At the end of the day players' careers were at stake and so was the integrity of the game – something I have always believed had to be upheld come what may.

There were a couple of occasions when I started umpiring that I felt the need to bollock a player who had overstepped the mark. I never did this on the field unless it was a very serious indiscretion but normally after the day's play. So a player would get a ticking-off from me and we'd resume the game and the other umpire would be chatting to said player, the incident would be mentioned, and my colleague wouldn't have the foggiest what he was on about. You can understand why certain umpires would get a bit resentful about this new kid on the block taking things into his own hands. So that was one of the first lessons I learned. Never fly solo because, as I quickly discovered, those one-on-one conversations could always be twisted, which potentially created even bigger issues. So, guys like Pete Willey and Mervyn Kitchen would put me right and I would always be grateful for their advice in my early years on the circuit.

Having played the game at a decent level definitely helped me but I had a lot of sympathy for some of my colleagues who hadn't played first-class cricket and whose ability as umpires were sometimes questioned as a result. One was Martin Bodenham, who was also from Sussex. I heard some poor feedback from players about Martin, along the same old themes that he didn't know the game because he had only played club cricket. I remember doing a game with him at Bristol and a player was having a go at him. I said, 'You do realise this guy refereed an FA Cup final? Don't you think he is capable of making good decisions?' Suddenly the players' demeanour changed and within a few weeks word had gone around the circuit that Martin, who'd done his time umpiring in the Sussex League, actually did know what he was doing. As far as I know he was never asked to referee one of the warm-up games of football most squads take part in before a day's play, but he was eventually accepted for what he was – a very good first-class umpire.

Anyway, I must have been doing something right for there I was at the Oval just shy of my 49th birthday umpiring a one-day international and I couldn't have had anyone better than Darrell Hair alongside me. He became my unofficial mentor when I got on the ICC panel and we clicked straightaway, probably because Darrell was as bad a judge of a racehorse as I was. I still find it a real shame all these years later that his career came to such a sad end in 2008, two years after Pakistan walked off the field at the Oval when Darrell caught them ball-tampering. Darrell was still looking out for me years later. I hooked up with him in Sydney, where he now lives, a few years back and he put me right on a few things after there had been some minor controversy in a series involving Australia that I had been standing in.

I was pretty nervous that day at the Oval, but the weather was good, the pitch was pancake-flat and the game, won convincingly by Sri Lanka thanks to a century from Sanath Jayasuriya, passed without much incident. There wasn't a single lbw decision in either innings and the most pressure I felt was when Jamie Dalrymple, a lad I'd brought into the Middlesex set-up from Radley College, was bowling or batting. I was probably more nervous for him, but he did get a few runs (37) and bowled tidily enough. More importantly, Darrell handed me a beer in the changing room afterwards and said: 'Well done.' Those encouraging words gave me so much confidence and I absolutely loved being on that stage: packed house, two good teams, world-class players. I really felt that I deserved to be there. I was underway.

Darrell was really good to me in that first series, but he knew when it was time to stop pissing about or picking that day's horses. A few weeks later I was at Lord's for another one-day international. Nigel Llong was standing with Darrell that day and I was third umpire. I was acting the fool a bit in the dressing room, taking my tie on and off because it was very warm and Nigel, who was new to the international circuit like me, and I felt we should not have to wear them because it was so hot. Darrell was about to walk down the stairs to go out when he spun on his heels and, with one or two expletives to reinforce his message, told us in no uncertain terms that if ICC were happy that we didn't wear ties we would be told. So ties it was. Darrell walked away, a somewhat chastened Nigel followed him and I sat down and absorbed another lesson. Have a laugh but know when to be serious.

I'm not sure if it was a deliberate ICC policy to see how much I wanted to do the job but in those first few months I umpired in some very different places. After the Sri Lanka series finished, I went to Toronto as a last-minute replacement for Daryl Harper, to do a couple of one-day internationals between Canada and Bermuda. It was the first time since I'd played against him in New Zealand in the early 1980s that I had come across Jeff Crowe, who was starting out as an ICC referee. I'd actually played in Canada in the 1970s for Derrick Robins XI, so I remembered the ground in Toronto. I must admit I thought ten days out there with two low-key games would be a bit of a jolly and to a certain extent it was because the cricket was pretty average. But a couple of hours with Jeff over a beer soon put me right on a few things: 'People are monitoring you all the time at ICC now, it doesn't matter whether you're here or at Lord's so concentrate hard on the games and don't let your standards slip.' Another lesson learned.

At home, I'd started what was basically a grass-cutting business and it was going pretty well. I used to cut sports fields around Berkshire and was quite happy whiling away a few hours sitting on the tractor going up and down. I found it therapeutic. Late in 2006 I was on a school playing field somewhere on a Friday afternoon when the phone rang. It was Sarah Edgar, who used to look after the umpires' arrangements at ICC.

'Ian, can you go and do an Intercontinental Cup game in Dubai?'

'No problem, when is it?'

'Tomorrow.'

I was such an eager beaver back then I didn't hesitate in agreeing to go. I drove home and packed a case while Jo ironed a few shirts before driving me to Heathrow. I flew out that night, got to Dubai at six o'clock their time the next morning and four hours later I was walking out to umpire a four-day match between United Arab Emirates and Scotland. A few weeks later, at the start of January 2007, I was in Mombasa in Kenya doing a triangular series involving the hosts, Canada and Scotland. Again, I had no hesitation in going even though Mombasa wasn't the sort of place where you could stroll out to take the evening air. It was the first time I'd been anywhere where there were blokes on the street carrying guns.

The feedback I got from ICC was that the reason they were sending me to places like Canada and Kenya was because they felt that English umpires, who earned a decent living with their domestic contract, were a bit soft. Neil Mallender left the international circuit at the time because of personal reasons but there was no danger I was going to walk away. I was enjoying it too much. I loved getting up in the morning because I knew I'd be doing something I wanted to do. If ICC had sent me to Siberia I'd have gone without hesitation.

Less than a year after my debut I was off to the 2007 World Cup in the West Indies. Thinking about it now, when I signed my first year-long contract I should have realised I'd be working at the tournament but when the list of umpires was confirmed I was gobsmacked. I had stood in fewer than ten international matches, not all of them very high profile, and here I was going to the biggest event in the game. I was away for nearly a month – way longer than any of the series I'd done before – and it turned out to be a big learning curve for me. I did Pakistan's warm-up games and although I only stood in three matches in the tournament itself, working with guys like Billy Bowden and Steve Bucknor was a real eye-opener.

I still get asked about Billy a lot. I knew him a bit from when I had played in New Zealand and I liked Billy, although he was a nervous wreck most of the time. He had become something of a celebrity, especially in places like India, because of his mannerisms and some people felt he had got bigger than the game. Billy was an outstanding decision-maker and had a heart of gold but I never had an inferiority complex when I stood with him, even back then when he was an established umpire and I was not.

One of my World Cup games was between Ireland and Zimbabwe when I stood with Brian Jerling and Billy was third umpire. That day, I felt Billy was taking the piss out of Brian. When Brian wanted confirmation there were two balls left in the over, Billy would tell him three, or if Brian thought the ball had hit the pad Billy would tell him there had been bat first, little things like that. Back then all the third umpire got involved in were line decisions, so you had a lot of time to observe, and the whole panorama of the ground to look at. It all came back to umpiring as a partnership and that was a bad day for Brian. Basically, Billy was undermining him and I thought he was out of order. So, at the end of the game, and to the evident surprise of Brian, I told Billy as much. If I hadn't known Billy from way back, I wouldn't have said anything but, to his credit, he accepted that he had overstepped the mark.

I loved umpiring at that World Cup, but it was overshadowed by the death of Bob Woolmer, someone I had known for years and had played against many times. I had been reserve umpire for Pakistan's infamous game against Ireland in Kingston which Ireland famously won by three wickets with all sorts of rumours flying around afterwards that the game had been fixed. I remember on the day there was lots of debate about Pakistan's decision to play an extra seamer when the wicket at Sabina Park was dry and spun like a top. They were 20-1 on favourites with the bookies, Ireland 8-1 against.

During Pakistan's warm-up games Bob, who was their coach, and I had a little routine where I'd meet with him in the hotel bar for the first drink of the evening. After losing to Ireland Bob was crushed, but we arranged as usual to have a drink in the swimming-pool bar at the Pegasus Hotel in Kingston. I was already there when I saw him come down in the lift and hold up his hand to indicate he'd be with me in five minutes. And that was the last time I saw him alive. When he didn't show I thought nothing of it but as the evening wore on all sorts of rumours started flying about that Bob had been taken ill. I then took a call from a reporter who asked whether I'd heard that he'd died of a heart attack. A few minutes later I saw him being taken out of the hotel in a body bag. Cricket lost a great man that day and I lost a mate. His death totally overshadowed the rest of the tournament for me.

A few days later I spoke to the British detective Mark Shields, who investigated Bob's death having been seconded from Scotland Yard to the Jamaican police force. It wasn't a formal interview as such but he admitted that the conspiracy theorists were having a field day. Bob had been taking medication for his diabetes and was under a lot of stress. Officially, the verdict was natural causes but even now, 13 years later, every time his name comes up another possible explanation is mentioned. Suicide? Poisoning? A victim of a hit man? We'll probably never know. He was writing a book at the time with the English journalist Ivo Tennant but that was about his coaching experiences, nothing else. His death was a great loss to the game and, more importantly, to his wife and children.

Back in the UK, in the summer of 2007 I did my biggest one-day series to date – England versus India. Rahul Dravid was India's captain and I got my first taste of life around the Indian 'bubble' with the massive media presence which followed the squad and the intense scrutiny their players were under, even away from home, but especially in England when the grounds normally had as many Indian supporters inside them as English fans.

Going back many years, there was always this theory in the game that away from home India were a soft touch. But Dravid, who'd been in the job since 2004, had started to toughen them up a bit. They had some fantastically talented players but guys like Gautam Gambhir could start an argument in an empty room. He didn't go looking for trouble, but he was part of a new generation of Indian stars who weren't going to lie down any more, especially away from home. That process continued when Duncan Fletcher took over as coach in 2011. I knew Duncan from way back when I played in Zimbabwe. He could come across as a bit cold and distant with his trademark floppy hat and shades – 'Inscrutable Duncan' I used to call him. But when he relaxed, he was a lovely guy to be around and extremely knowledgeable about cricket and cricketers. That England–India series was a long one – seven matches in total with England winning 4-3 – and I also did India's warm-up game against Scotland in Glasgow, so I got to know the Indian players fairly well. I felt I'd had a good series, but it was still a surprise when a few weeks later I was appointed for their home series against Pakistan.

I'd never been to India before but I was warned that it could be a bit chaotic and in that regard I got a first taste of Indian timekeeping when I landed at Delhi airport at 2am and there was no one there to meet me and take me to the venue for the first match in Guwahati. Eventually someone turned up, after I'd rung Sarah Edgar and woke her up in the middle of the night. I'm not sure what people thought as I turned out my bag in the arrivals lounge at Delhi airport trying to find a contact number for Sarah, but it did teach me to be more prepared.

I found India a brilliant place to work in. The passion of the people for the game of cricket is unparalleled regardless of how well their team is doing. I remember looking out of my hotel room, which was next to the stadium in Guwahati, the night before the first one-day international and there was a queue of fans waiting for the gates to open as far as I could see, thousands of people bedding down for the night – well, lying on the ground – to make sure they could get in the next day. I was told the attendance was 40,000 and I don't think too many of them had waited until the morning of the match before they made their way to the stadium.

This wasn't any old series of course. It was India v Pakistan and included an infamous bust-up between Gambhir and Shahid Afridi which happened in the third match of the series in Kanpur. It caught me completely unawares. There was a fierce rivalry, but the games had been pretty tame until then with both sides winning once each heading into the third match.

India were struggling a bit and when Gambhir came out to bat at no.3 he immediately went on the attack, hitting Afridi through mid-on for four. A few words were exchanged, not much else. Gambhir then got a leading edge and the ball squirted out into the covers. As Afridi appealed, he stood his ground and dropped his shoulder and the two collided. More verbals, and this time I got hold of Pakistan's captain Shoaib Malik and effectively gave him and Afridi a final warning before telling Gambhir in no uncertain terms to calm down. By then the crowd were going apoplectic but that was only the start. A few moments later they came together again, and Afridi put his hand in Gambhir's visor and appeared to be shaking it like a dog with a plastic toy in its mouth. Somehow, I managed to smooth things over again but it was a pretty terrifying moment especially as they were both speaking in Urdu and I hadn't got a clue what they were saying.

After it quietened down a bit I looked over at my partner – Amiesh Saheba – at square leg and he hadn't moved. The match referee was Roshan Mahanama and at the break Amiesh admitted he hadn't seen any of the incidents. I found that more than a bit strange, but I had no concerns. The third umpire – a chap called Suresh Shastri – had videoed the game so the plan was to move on to Lucknow where we were staying overnight before I flew home the next day. We would watch the footage before Roshan could decide on what punishment to impose.

On the way to Lucknow, Malcolm Speed, who was ICC's chief executive at the time, chewed Roshan's ears off about getting it sorted as soon as possible as he was under a lot of pressure to come down hard on an incident which hardly showed the game in a good light. Eventually we got to the hotel where the Indian players were also staying, and MS Dhoni had organised a bit of a party to which we had all been invited. We all filed into my chalet and put the tape in the video recorder but all we could see on the screen were fuzzy lines. I thought there must be something wrong with the TV set so we went into another chalet and it was exactly the same. I called the hotel maintenance guy who tested the machine with another video and got a perfect picture. It turned out poor old Suresh hadn't turned the machine on at the ground so we couldn't have any sort of hearing until the authorities were able to get hold of pictures from the broadcasters which we knew would take a couple of days.

I flew home in the meantime and was told I'd be linked up to give evidence by video conference call when I got back to the UK. But there was another communication breakdown when they tried to call me and I couldn't hear or see a thing. In my opinion both players should have had the book thrown at them, but instead they were only fined a portion of their match fee which was ridiculously lenient. Gambhir eventually copped a one-Test ban after barging into Shane Watson a year later during a series against Australia.

I umpired nine India versus Pakistan games in my career and apart from that day in Kanpur I never had an issue with either team. Sure, the stakes were high, and you had to concentrate really hard. For me, that meant trying to block out the activities of the crowd. I never looked at what was going on in the stands, just straight ahead down the pitch or at the players if I was standing at square leg. The only time it was a problem was if the spectators started a Mexican wave when the noise would be deafening, and you would struggle to concentrate. As everyone knows,

Indians are passionate about cricket. There would always be a crowd of them outside the hotel where we stayed and some of the umpires became almost as big a celebrity as some of the players. Billy Bowden, for one, advertised a few products on Indian TV. I hated all that of course but I found if I changed my glasses – I always had four different pairs with me when I went to India – and shoved a baseball cap on I could go incognito.

Finally, in 2008 I stood in my first Test series. It was a fairly quiet introduction – two one-sided matches between South Africa and Bangladesh which a strong South African team won convincingly. The first Test was in Bloemfontein and only went into a fourth day because rain washed out the third. Alan Hurst was the referee, an Australian who was a real stickler for the regulations, and I stood with Steve Davis, who was such good company that I turned down the opportunity to fly home for a few days during the series so I could enjoy the craic with Steve. He told me that I had done well but added a caveat: 'Don't think every series is like this.'

People often ask me what the hardest place to umpire was. Physically, the toughest conditions were in Sri Lanka. The heat and humidity are off the scale and some days in Colombo, Kandy or Galle I would walk off at lunch and my feet were literally sloshing about in my socks and shoes because they were so wet with sweat. When I started, even in really hot and sunny places, I never wore sunglasses, although I always wore a wide-brimmed hat. But I remember talking to an optician called Bill Hatton before I went to Sri Lanka to do a series there in 2011 who warned me about how harsh the glare from the sunlight was. He gave me a couple of pairs of sunglasses but I only took them to be polite. I had no intention of wearing them until the first time I stepped out of my hotel in a place called Hambantota, looked at the pavement and felt my eyes burning because of the glare. After that, I always had a pair of sunglasses with me.

Coldest place? Well, Headingley in 2007 when I was third umpire for England versus West Indies took some beating. There was a big hole in the floor of our box through which the broadcasters could thread TV cables and I have never been as cold on a cricket ground as I was for those few days. It was one of the few times I felt sorry for the players. The West Indies lads emptied their bags to find as many layers as they could to put on and I don't think the temperature got into double figures at any time during the match.

Hobart could be parky too, especially if you went early in the Australian season. I remember doing a very cold Test match there in 2015 when, again, West Indies were the visitors and were clearly not enjoying the experience very much.

Pakistan was a bit like India, the fans absolutely loved their cricket and it's a shame teams did not go there for a number of years. The security situation is such that it is only now, more than a decade later, that they can consider hosting proper series in their country after the incident in 2009 when Sri Lanka's team bus was attacked by terrorists in Lahore. I was on stand-by for that series but a couple of days out was told I wasn't needed. I remember watching the drama all unfold on TV. One of my biggest mates in the game, Steve Davis, along with Simon Taufel and the match referee Chris Broad, were on the bus. I didn't realise that the pictures were live so I rang Steve to check he was okay. About three hours later he called me back to assure me he was fine. 'I saw your number on my phone Gunner,' he said. 'Trouble was I was lying in the middle of a bus at the time trying not to be shot!'

After a couple of years or so in the job I felt settled, part of the furniture. And it wasn't long before

I was handing down advice to some of the new recruits on the elite panel, guys like Richard Kettleborough who is now regarded as one of the best in the world at his job. I got the impression that the ICC were still a bit worried that, if I had a bad series, I would walk away but I was in it for the long haul. I still made mistakes. I remember a series in Sri Lanka against Pakistan in 2012 when, between Steve Davis and I, we made 15 wrong decisions, we couldn't buy one. That's why you used to pray to be appointed for series in Australia, New Zealand or South Africa where the wickets are pretty true. If it went wrong then you put your hand up but when the ball was turning and spitting all over the shop you were never going to get every decision right, no matter how good you felt your judgement was.

Most of the guys practised, as I did, back then. At the end of the day everyone's preparation is different, and it didn't worry me if the other umpire wasn't bothered about coming to stand in the nets with me, that was their choice. I even did it when I was third umpire, just in case one of my colleagues fell ill and I had to stand in for them. They were long days, often in hot conditions, but the more I did the job the fitter I became. I loved walking, I never got a bus or taxi to the ground if I could stroll there and if I couldn't do that I'd walk for an hour on a treadmill, just to clear my mind. I was having an absolute blast. This was what I wanted to do.

4

Man Management

IT may have been because I played for England, but I never felt in awe of the players, some of whom were among the best the world had ever seen, when I umpired at the elite end of the game. Obviously, things were a lot different when I played for England. The levels of professionalism are off the scale now compared to the early 1980s, but the fundamentals of the game are still the same. Bowl ball, hit ball, catch ball.

As an umpire, man management was always my strongest point. Not decision-making. In that regard I was as good or as bad as any of my colleagues. I have made more than my fair share of howlers but the only time I was ever verbally abused on the pitch for a decision I made came in 2019, and a few weeks after I'd stood in my last international match. In a T20 Blast game at Bristol I punished Gloucestershire with six penalty runs for a slow over rate and they went on to lose a tight one to Sussex by three wickets in the last over. My fellow umpire Michael Burns and I had made a mistake because we waited until the end of the over before confirming the punishment when we should have done it during the middle of the over when Gloucestershire ran out of time. I should have known the regulation and not put Michael, one of the best of the next generation of English umpires, in a difficult position as a result.

Anyway, the home captain Michael Klinger – who'd played a lot of cricket in his career including several matches for Australia – let me have it. Not to my face, but from 15 yards away, which I thought was poor. I was so surprised I was lost for words on a cricket field for probably the only time in 30-plus years. It wasn't our fault that Gloucestershire bowled their overs too slowly.

Right from when I started on the international panel in 2006 I was determined to be open and approachable on the field. I would need another book to detail the number of times I had to defuse a potentially difficult situation with a strong word, or an offer to listen to the gripes of the players involved after play to find some common ground and make sure there was no lingering dissent for the rest of the match or series. In every international there is a lot at stake. Careers of players and coaches can be on the line and I understood that. But after a couple of years on the circuit I felt players understood me. I'd talk to anyone. But if they crossed the line and I thought something wasn't right they would get an earful.

My method was always to try to nip things in the bud. At the end of an over, I would never walk to square leg until the wicketkeeper and slips had jogged past me because that's when the best sledgers – and in my time there was none better than Australia's wicketkeeper Brad Haddin – did their best work on the non-striker. If you wandered off to square leg with your back to the players, you could miss an awful lot.

I was also fortunate in some ways to have the attention span of a gnat. Of course umpires need to have good concentration levels – but they are only needed when the bowler is running in and the batsman is preparing to face. Between deliveries I would look at someone or something in the crowd just to take my mind off things. But as soon as I heard the bowler turn from his mark and start to run in, I switched on. The other advantage of that is you heard what was going on around you, like stupid remarks by mid-on or mid-off to the non-striker. If you were staring down the wicket and that was your only focus you would be oblivious to all that peripheral stuff that went on.

The thing about good players and something that can definitely be applied to great players is that they don't miss the ball very often. If the pitch was flat and the bounce is true you knew you wouldn't have to make many difficult decisions during the course of a Test match or one-day game. It has become hard work for international bowlers in recent years, and I suppose the balance has only swung back towards them since the advent of DRS. Grounds all over the world dry so quickly these days that you very rarely encounter a really poor wicket. The ball might spin a lot in places like Sri Lanka and Bangladesh, so you have to have your wits about you, but in most other countries, once they get themselves established, high-quality batsmen are only going to get themselves out by making a mistake.

So it can be hard work for bowlers, especially fast bowlers operating on unresponsive wickets, often with a Kookaburra ball in places like Australia and South Africa which goes flat after 25 overs or so. The quicks can get frustrated and when that happens as an umpire you have to be able to spot the signs and, if necessary, do something about it.

A classic example of the big fast bowler who often felt wronged was the Australian Ryan Harris, a highly skilled operator whose career was sadly blighted by injuries. In 2010 Australia were playing New Zealand in Wellington and poor old Ryan – who, off the field, is one of the nicest guys I have ever met – was getting increasingly exasperated. I remember walking back to his mark with him on a couple of occasions trying to calm him down because I sensed a big explosion was coming. I told him if he was looking for the match referee to nick him he was going the right way about it. I certainly didn't want to finish the day in cricket's equivalent of the headmaster's study when I could have been draining a cold beer and eventually the penny dropped.

A year later my coach Denis Burns was working at the Under-19 World Cup in Bangladesh and he retold me a story that I am still very proud of. The umpires for the tournament were sitting with the captains and coaches in a pre-series workshop. Denis was there with three young umpires, the Australian captain Will Sutherland, the manager Graham Manou and their coach Ryan Harris.

The discussion was based around communication and how umpires can manage the game by supporting players in non-confrontational ways. Ryan gave an example: 'Gunner Gould helped me a lot as a player. When I was mad, he spoke to me. He was subtle and nobody else knew he was talking to me, not even my captain. He sometimes walked a few paces back with me when I was walking back to my mark. He'd ask me to calm down and let him take care of the batsman who was winding me up. I respected him because he always did what was in the best interests of the game. That's what I mean by communication.'

Back in the early stages of my international career, it was too easy for match referees to throw the book at players. When they were first introduced by ICC it was considered something of a cushy number. They basically threw the coin in the air at the toss and then sat back and enjoyed the cricket. But as coverage of the game intensified, particularly after the advent of DRS, there was very little that happened that TV cameras didn't pick up. It didn't mean, though, that you had to agree with every decision a referee made. I remember a Test match in Perth in 2009 when Sueliman Benn, the West Indies spinner, barged into Mitchell Johnson as he tried to field the ball and Brad

Haddin predictably joined in with the verbals. None of them came out of the incident with much credit but Benn got banned for two games. I thought it was a ridiculous overreaction and refused to sign the charge sheet. Chris Broad, the match referee, wasn't happy but I was never carpeted by the ICC over it.

If you found out about players, especially those you hadn't come across before, and did your homework it tended to make life so much easier. And I always made my own mind up rather than making assumptions based on what I'd heard. A classic example of this was MS Dhoni, one of India's greatest-ever players. He's such a powerful figure, not just in Indian cricket but worldwide, that you picked a fight with him at your peril. I'd been warned that he could be hard work and wanted to run the game rather than letting the umpires do their job, but I think he's one of the nicest guys I've ever come across in cricket. Look, if he thought something was wrong he would be the first person to bang on your door at the end of the day and say why but he was always polite and he never stitched me up.

If you spoke to people you trusted when you were going to encounter players for the first time it tended to make life a lot easier. Again, another example of good preparation. Before I umpired Australia for the first time after Ricky Ponting was made captain, during a one-day series against South Africa in 2009, I got hold of Justin Langer, someone I knew from his spell in county cricket with Middlesex when I was coaching there. 'What's he like, Justin?' I asked. 'Don't bullshit him, and if you do, make sure when you're doing it that you're looking him straight in the eye,' was Justin's typically no-nonsense response.

We were in Melbourne for the series opener and I turned down a close lbw. At the end of the over Ricky ran towards me from slip and asked why it wasn't out. I took my glasses off, looked him square in the eye and said: 'I thought it was going down mate, if it wasn't, I'm sorry.' I held my gaze for several more seconds, determined that the first person who blinked wasn't going to be me. Eventually Ricky cracked a big smile. 'You've been speaking to Langer, haven't you?'

Now, it's common knowledge that Ricky, like myself, enjoys a flutter, hence his nickname Punter. We were chatting during a game later in that series in Hobart when he told me he had a dog running that evening in Launceston. A dead cert he said. Anyway, I toddled off to the dog track and Ricky's dead cert was so slow I think it ended up being lapped by the hare. I lost a few quid but thought nothing more about it. The series moved on to Sydney and when Australia were in the field I approached Ricky at the end of an over. I knew the cameras were on us because I could see the big screen out of the corner of my eye. I told him his tips were as bad as mine, but he gave me the name of another dog or horse which was a sure thing and I wrote it down in my notebook. After the game the match referee Ranjan Madugalle was in a right state as he made a beeline for me in the umpires' room. The press had seen us stern-faced, arms outstretched on the screens and wanted to know what the argument was all about. All I had been doing was telling Ricky that I thought his hopeless greyhound was still running around in circles in Launceston!

By then, three years into the job, I felt I was on top of my game but in 2010 came a reality check from an unlikely source. I've always thought that the leading cricket writers know as much or more about the game and what makes players tick as anyone else, even if they haven't played at a high level, and I always tried to maintain a good relationship with reporters wherever I was in the world. It helps that most of them like a pint.

I was doing New Zealand versus Australia and, in those pre-DRS days when the pressure wasn't as intense, I felt I was umpiring out of my boots. And I was having a good time off the field as well. I'd played against Peter Roebuck and had a few run-ins with him when we were captains of Sussex and Somerset before he made his life in Australia and became a very fine cricket writer. Peter wasn't everyone's cup of tea, but I respected his opinion. One night in Wellington he came over in a bar and said that a few of the Australian journalists felt I was socialising too much. 'They're gunning for you Ian,' he told me. Because we'd had one or two arguments in the dim and distant past I might have been forgiven if I'd told him to get stuffed, but deep down I knew he was right. I liked to unwind in the evening with a drink but after that warning I steered away from hotel bars or other places where players liked to congregate, and I pulled my head in a bit. He was right. I was umpiring so well then that I almost felt I wouldn't make a mistake.

I'd got complacent which was a state of mind I didn't expect because for the vast majority of my career there was always this little voice in the back of my head telling me not to fuck things up. I was enjoying the lifestyle too much, even the travelling. It was only in the last 18 months before I retired from international umpiring that I didn't have the same enthusiasm on the drive to Gatwick or Heathrow that I used to have.

We're all fallible though, aren't we? But until my mental health issues in 2015-16 I never allowed it to grind me down. If I had a bad day I would come off, sit in the corner quietly, smoke a couple of cigarettes, and half an hour later I'd be fine. I never holed up in a hotel room after I'd had a stinker – I always made the effort to socialise for an hour or so before getting an early night.

In one respect, umpiring has become less pressurised since DRS because there is no hiding place now. Any errors will get picked up by the technology, debated on TV and then dissected on social media for hours afterwards. But it's soon old news and the cricket agenda moves on, with the next important match or series never too far away. When I started, the only evidence was the naked eye or TV cameras and back then there wasn't the depth of coverage there is now with any number of camera angles available. If you didn't feel the players trusted you to make sound decisions consistently you were on a slippery slope and the next series couldn't come around soon enough.

During my 13 years the player–umpire relationship has changed for two main reasons: DRS and the proliferation of T20 tournaments around the world when sworn enemies in a Test series can, a few weeks later, become best buddies and team-mates in the Indian Premier League (IPL) or Big Bash. Suddenly, they all knew each other's business and the clever ones would try to use it to their advantage the next time they were in opposition in an international arena. I climbed into players many times because I thought their behaviour, choice of language or reference to an opponent's family overstepped the mark only to be reassured: 'It's okay Gunner, we're fine, we know each other from the IPL.'

Incidentally, my own international commitments meant it wasn't until 2018 that I did the IPL for the first time and I absolutely loved it. Considering what was at stake, and the intensity of the media scrutiny, I was astonished at how good player behaviour was. The IPL was a real bucket-list moment for me, even if the early-morning or late-night travelling was tough at times. The atmosphere in the grounds was amazing, the standard of cricket very high and I came across players I'd never met before. It was a brilliant experience.

Who wouldn't have enjoyed having the best view in the house when some of the greatest batsmen in the history of the game were in full flow? Who was the best player I umpired? I'm asked that a lot and it is hard for me to look beyond Sachin Tendulkar. Standing there, waiting for him to emerge from a dressing room anywhere in the world, not just India, to come out and bat – I didn't experience anything like it. The noise levels went from funereal silence to a deafening roar in a matter of seconds. Whenever Sachin took guard I always used to gesture with my hands because shouting at him was pointless. Even 22 yards away he wouldn't have heard a thing.

As I mentioned, good players don't miss the ball too often and I only gave him out once lbw – and that was overturned on review. It was during the 2011 World Cup semi-final against Pakistan when he was facing the off-spinner Saeed Ajmal. I thought the ball was smacking all three stumps over, and Sachin had to be persuaded by Gautam Gambhir to review it, but he did and it was overturned. Sachin went on to make 85 and India won and, as always with him, at the end of the game he shook my hand and thanked me.

Other players I enjoyed watching? Virender Sehwag springs to mind because, on his day, he was capable of dismantling any attack in the world. Jacques Kallis, the supreme South African all-rounder, was another I loved seeing bat and so, on his day, was Hashim Amla. When you see these guys play a great shot it's sometimes hard not to join in the applause!

For me, the one thing that sets the finest players apart from the rest – and I'm talking about modern-day greats like Virat Kohli, Kane Williamson and Steve Smith – is their practice and preparation. They might kick a football around for a couple of minutes to loosen up, but in the nets they are always deadly serious. They make the pace bowlers send it down as quickly as they can, and they will only stop sessions to perhaps ask a coach a question if something doesn't feel right. Apart from that, they adopt the same attitude in the nets as they would in a match situation. When he is in full flow, as we saw in the 2019 Ashes, Steve Smith is a genius. I don't think any other word describes how good he is.

And their standards never drop. Every time I saw Virat, Kane or Steve the day before a game, and Sachin Tendulkar was the same earlier in my umpiring career, the intensity levels would be the same. The nearest equivalent among England players is Ben Stokes, whom I saw practise as hard as anyone during the

Indian Premier League in 2018. These guys obviously have fantastic ability as well, but they are so driven and set their personal standards very high.

Sometimes, if Virat was not sure about something during a game, he would occasionally ask me. Seriously. More than once in games where I have umpired him, after he has scratched around for four or five overs, he has asked me if everything looks right. Now, I never had anywhere near the ability of someone like him, Kane Williamson or Steve Smith but after all these years in cricket, including nearly a decade coaching Middlesex, I still think I can spot flaws in technique quite quickly. Usually, it's their hands which aren't moving properly or in the right place. Once, I said to Virat, 'Do you want to bat like Virat Kohli or Ian Gould?' and suggested he made a tiny adjustment to the position of his bottom hand on the bat. He agreed, and within a few minutes was back to his old self. Which is great for me too, because I loved watching guys like him bat for as long as possible.

The other thing to mention about Virat is that he loves his statistics. He knows what's going on in the world game almost as soon as it's happened. He would sometimes ask my opinion about an up-and-coming young player and then give me chapter and verse on their career so far. He also knew about the greats of the past because he listened to old players and their assessments of different players in different eras.

It probably is a batsman's game these days and you can almost forgive bowlers who try anything to gain an advantage with the ball. When I played, ball-tampering was extremely primitive. We all knew certain players tried it and we all knew about their rudimentary methods, which sometimes involved scratching the surface with the side of a beer-bottle top. These days it's done a lot more covertly and has almost become a skill in itself. As an umpire you have to be so careful before you effectively start accusing someone of cheating. With the all-seeing eye of TV there's not much players can get away with anyway and, as we found in Cape Town in 2018, when it goes wrong it can ruin players' careers. I have stood many times and seen the ball hoop around and thought that can't have happened without some work on the ball, only to be thrown it at the end of an over and discover not even a blemish on its surface.

I remember a one-day international series against West Indies in India in 2014. The ball kept coming back with marks all over it which I thought had been made by someone's fingernails. We had our suspicions, but we weren't alerted to anything untoward. The day before the next match in Delhi I was at practice and during throw-downs the ball kept hitting the LED advertising boards. When the session finished, I picked up a ball lying in front of the boards and it looked as if someone had been at it with razor blades. You really have to be absolutely sure before accusing someone and in one-day internationals now, when two balls are in use, it's a lot easier to check the ball while I've never believed a T20 is a long enough game for tampering to make a difference.

Having said all that, I was involved in two of the biggest ball-tampering incidents within the space of a few months towards the end of my career. The furore surrounding Sandpaper-gate early in 2018 had hardly died down when I headed out to the West Indies for their series against South Africa that summer. After what had gone on in Cape Town, I was looking forward to a few pleasant weeks in the Caribbean with Aleem Dar, Richard Kettleborough and the match referee Javagal Srinath. You might have thought both teams would have been on their best behaviour as well. I've never had a problem with West Indies and while you sometimes didn't know what to expect from Sri Lanka, the pre-series meeting left us with no indication that there would be any issues.

West Indies won the first Test and we moved on to St Lucia. On the second day Aleem and I raised concerns with Javagal about the condition of the ball. An eagle-eyed cameraman spotted Dinesh Chandimal, Sri Lanka's captain, chewing a sweet and then applying saliva to it. He alerted us after the day's play, although when we had seen the ball at the end of play it was hard to work out whether it had been tampered with. With the video evidence provided, we were within our rights to challenge that they had attempted to change the condition of the ball.

To say Chandimal didn't take this accusation well would be an understatement. He told us he wasn't sure what he'd been chewing, which we found amusing. On the third day we got to the ground to discover that Sri Lanka were effectively on strike. When Aleem and I walked out at 10.30am to get the game underway we were accompanied by the two West Indies batsmen and no one else. We turned around and walked back towards the pavilion where I found Dinesh on his phone, talking to a member of their board of control. We tried a second time.

Again, no Sri Lanka players. Eventually, two hours later under threat from us of forfeiting the Test, they agreed to play.

When play had finished, we had Chandimal, coach Chandika Hathurusingha and team manager Asanka Gurusinha in for a chat. We had made one mistake. When Javagal had questioned Chandimal after day two there had been no witnesses to the conversation. Effectively it was his word against Chandimal's. And now Chandimal, whom I'd had many conversations in English with down the years, complained that he didn't understand what was going on as he couldn't speak English!

Sri Lanka got away lightly. Chandimal was banned from the final Test in Bridgetown, the coach and manager charged with 'conduct that was contrary to the spirit of the game'. I was fuming. If it had been up to me, I'd have abandoned the Test and awarded it to West Indies. It was totally unfair on their players. The ironic thing is that Sri Lanka would probably have won the game but for the time lost to their ridiculous protest. I just couldn't get my head around why they thought they would get away with it, especially in the wake of what had happened a few weeks earlier in South Africa. It was piss-poor all round and, not for the first time, I felt ICC's decision-making was shown to be too lenient.

Sometimes, though, I struggle to understand the thought processes of players. One of the worst periods I experienced during my umpiring career was at the end of 2014 when I heard that Phil Hughes had died after being struck on the neck during a Sheffield Shield match at the Sydney Cricket Ground. I was devastated. I'd first come across Phil when he played briefly for Middlesex in county cricket but it was earlier that year, when Australia played South Africa and the host country Zimbabwe in a one-day series, that I got to know him very well.

He came up to me in the hotel bar in Harare early one evening and asked to borrow a razor so he could have a shave. I thought nothing of it and gave him my room key. A few hours later I went back to the room to discover the bed and chair missing. With the help of a couple of bemused hotel porters, he'd relocated them to the storeroom. I should have been furious, but I actually found it very funny. I think Aaron Finch had told him I'd probably take it well. We had a lot of chats over those couple of weeks. There wasn't much to do in Zimbabwe at the time away from the hotel and we got along famously.

So my initial thoughts after I'd heard of his death was that there was no way Australia's impending series against India would take place. But the two boards agreed that it was the best way to honour Phil's memory, so I flew out with Jo. I was in Adelaide when his funeral took place and it was like a state occasion. Jo went off shopping and I found a perch in a bar somewhere, had a beer and cried my eyes out, a very rare show of emotion for me. It was one of the lowest periods in my career. Seeing his family and the Australian cricketers mourning their loss had a powerful effect on me. So much so that I got horrendously lost trying to walk back to the hotel and Jo had to come and find me a few hours later.

The start of the series was delayed and there was a frightening incident at practice a couple of days before the first Test when Peter Siddle hit Shane Watson on the head. It happens a lot in the nets and people get on with it but after what happened to Phil there was almost an air of paranoia. Luckily Shane was fine, and I thought the Indian players and management showed remarkable respect for their opponents in the lead-up to the game.

For the first couple of days the atmosphere was very sombre. Steve Smith scored a brilliant century and how he handled the emotion of the occasion earned him a lot of respect from me. It must have been incredibly difficult merely for Steve to take the field, as he and Phil were incredibly close. The applause for his hundred must have gone on for about three minutes while I stood there, taking it all in and trying to hold back the tears. But by day three it was business as usual. The tensions that inevitably come to the surface when these two sides meet had been bubbling away and finally exploded when David Warner got out to Varun Aaron and the Indian bowler gave him a right royal send-off.

But we'd spotted that Aaron had overstepped and Warner was recalled and all hell broke loose. Shane Watson got involved, Shikhar Dhawan had his say and then later in the day Steve Smith took exception to what was a very optimistic lbw appeal from Rohit Sharma which I had turned down. Kohli and Smith had a face-off, which my colleague Marais Erasmus had to defuse. The funny thing is that when Virat Kohli had been hit on the helmet earlier in the match it was Warner who was the first person to check on him. There must have been some leftovers from when the Australians had played in the IPL, but it made for three very challenging days when I felt the players would have been on their best behaviour. We managed the situation well I thought, but I was staggered by what went on bearing in mind what happened in the build-up.

Nine months after Cape Town in 2018 I was umpiring Australia again, in a home series against India. Two of the top sides in the world, Australia at home for the first time since Sandpaper-gate and anxious to prove to their cricket public that they were playing the game the right way. Well, that's what I imagined as I flew out to Melbourne for the Boxing Day Test with Jo.

By then I knew it was probably going to be the last time I stood in a series involving two of the powers of world cricket. Needless to say, I only arrived for the third and fourth Tests. In Melbourne I stood with the South African umpire Marais Erasmus and then in Sydney with Richard Kettleborough. That was fine because, as it turned out, without Steve Smith and David Warner Australia behaved on the field impeccably. But still? Why had me, Ketts and Erasmus not been standing for the first two Tests? Three experienced umpires who could have set the tempo for the rest of the series. ICC clearly hadn't learned their lessons from the South Africa fiasco and, after the Ashes, this series was as big as it gets.

Look, it's been an absolute joy and privilege to stand with some of these guys. But on other occasions I did wonder what the ICC were thinking when they drew up appointments for certain series. And I don't necessarily mean umpires either. Guys like Andy Pycroft, who was with us again for that Australia–India series, are superb match referees but some of the others are scared of their own shadow. They are too worried that if they upset players it's going to affect their chances of being involved in lucrative gigs like the IPL. There are quite a few match referees and umpires who would have struggled to cope with what happened in Cape Town, and not because they lacked experience.

I'm not perfect – I know that. I've made mistakes but I always umpired – whether it was Australia v India or a schools' finals day at Hove – in the same way I expected to be umpired as a player. Be fair, be honest but if you cross the line I will tell you. But I have lost count of the occasions when I have asked my fellow umpire to confirm that he has ticked off a player, more often than not on the subcontinent, about an indiscretion on the field and had an assurance that he had, only to discover a few hours later, having spoken to said player myself, that no such conversation had ever taken place.

India runs the world game – not England or Australia – I get that. If it means missing out on a few weeks at the IPL are you seriously going to tell someone like Virat Kohli that he or his team have gone too far? I can understand their apprehension. But that doesn't make it right in my book. When the shit hits the fan, too many umpires in my opinion have kept well away from trouble and the ICC have never acted quickly enough to get to grips with the issue. And I don't see it changing much in the future if I'm honest.

Anyway, Justin Langer had taken over from Darren Lehmann as Australia coach for the India series and, as far as I was concerned, that was a positive step. The media's investigation into what happened at Cape Town was very thorough, but it did surprise me that it took until the eve of the final Test before the coach resigned. Look, I like Darren. I umpired him many times when he was playing for Yorkshire and admired him as a player, he was one of the best batsmen we had in the county game during the first half of this century. But I firmly believe that the coach sets the tempo for the team and in South Africa in 2018 Darren's team went way too far.

Justin is what I call a proper bloke. Not only was he a brilliant batsman but, after he took up coaching, he set similarly high standards. I've had many a pint with him after play and I liked his way of thinking. When I heard he had become Australia coach I knew they were in good hands and I thought the way he conducted himself during the Ashes series in 2019 was outstanding. He might not come across that way, but Justin is actually quite a humorous fellow. But I wouldn't want to get on the wrong side of him. He's very principled. The game needs more people like him in positions of influence.

And there is no doubt in my mind that Australia's behaviour since Cape Town has improved. They had been out of control and I don't think anyone around the team at that time would deny it. But ICC and to a certain extent the umpires, including myself, should have nailed them earlier. It only takes one or two bad apples to ruin things.

My personal view is that it started when Ricky Ponting was no longer captain after 2012 because he commanded enormous respect in their squad and, if you remember, there were some very big characters in the Australian team during the time when he was in charge. I remember doing a Test in Perth towards the end of his career when Ricky was hit by Kemar Roach, the West Indies fast bowler. That was very unlike him because in my experience he always played fast bowling very well. I sensed then that his physical powers might be just starting to decline, and that was in 2009, three years before he retired. I didn't think anyone in the team could take the team on and lead it the way he had and we saw what happened as a result as their on-field behaviour deteriorated.

However, they should have been pulled into line long before Cape Town happened. By the time they settled their pay dispute with the Australian board, after losing a Test to Bangladesh in 2017, they were on a course which ended in the dramatic way it did against South Africa in 2018.

I did what turned out to be my penultimate Test match in Sydney at the start of 2019. During 13 years as an umpire I think I spent two Christmases at home which suited me just fine, as I'm not a big fan of the festivities. I always preferred to be in Melbourne or Cape Town, watching the world go by for a few days in nice weather before doing the match. Jo used to ring me because she was worried that I'd be lonely. Most of the time I was the happiest man in the world.

5

Burnt Out

THERE is a misconception about me. On the field of play I used to make it my business to interact with the players, try to keep smiling even when things were getting a bit heated and not come over as officious and bossy. It was a different way of umpiring compared to a lot of my colleagues, but it was my way and, over the best part of 20 years, 13 of them on the international circuit, it has worked.

I was the same off the field except when the conversation got around to cricket. That was the last thing I wanted to talk about when I was unwinding with a drink after a day's play. I remember having some smashing chats with Mickey Arthur when he was South Africa coach about his favourite (and my favourite) English football team, Arsenal. We'd sit there for hours talking about the Gunners and the merits of our favourite players. Then one day Mickey made a big mistake. He began talking about the game we were involved in and I walked away, pint in hand. 'Where are you going, Gunner?' he shouted as I disappeared back to my room. Someone later told him that I hated talking about cricket away from the game and after that little misunderstanding Mickey and I got on as well as we always had.

My cricket time was when I was at the ground or when we were travelling to the venue. You wouldn't get much conversation out of me in that hour or so before play is due to start. But once I crossed the boundary rope, I was off and that was where I wanted to be. After play, I would go back to the hotel, get showered and changed and be out again in ten minutes. Look, we're all made differently. Some of my colleagues were quite happy to sit in their rooms, have a bit of food, watch some TV, ring the family and go to bed. I was never one for late nights, but I did like to unwind and socialise. And when I did meet up with other umpires, I found the ones who had come into the international game having had a career away from cricket much more interesting.

On days off, whether I was in Kandy, Cape Town or Christchurch, I would take off in the morning and not come back until later in the evening. I'd walk for miles, wandering into random bars and just chatting to the locals over a drink. I never told them what I did, and because I was a master of disguise with my various hats, caps and different pairs of glasses, I could get away with being incognito. And if anyone asked me what I did, I told them I was a groundsman which was true for most of the time I umpired at the elite level. It was only in the last few years that my youngest son George had fully taken over the groundsman business I set up while I was coaching Middlesex. It wasn't a lie. Well, I suppose it was a small lie. Even when I was back in England, socialising with my pals at home, I always drank in a pub which wasn't showing cricket on TV so I couldn't watch my umpiring colleagues making mistakes or have my own errors dissected by the pundits. My friends knew that the last thing I wanted to natter about was cricket.

To be honest I'm a loner. You might wonder how someone who has been married for more than 30 years actually prefers his own company. And I ask myself that regularly, believe me! When I met Jo I was playing for Sussex and she very soon got used to the fact that I was away from home a lot. Not much changed when I went into coaching and certainly not when I became an international umpire. When I joined the panel in 2006 Gemma was 20, Michael 17 and George 14 so they had been brought up with their dad being away from home for long periods. And they loved their own space too. The biggest issue was when I came back from an overseas trip. For the first three or four days I'd be back in the swing of things – taking Jo out, or running the kids here, there and everywhere – but, when the jet lag kicked in, I'd be good for nothing. Jo has been an absolute rock for me but now and again she flew off the handle, frustrated that when I came home all I wanted to do was put my feet up and wait until my next overseas assignment.

But the family put up with it for two reasons. They knew it was something I loved to do, and they occasionally enjoyed the perks of coming on trips with me. I think the only country Jo never visited while I was umpiring was India. She'd heard some bad stories about the country so she wasn't keen despite the fact that I kept telling her it was one of my favourite places to go. She regretted that at the time but now I am off the treadmill I will take her and show her what a fantastic country it is.

One year I worked out that I'd spent just 80 nights at home that year because of domestic and international commitments, as well as the umpires' seminars you had to attend at ICC headquarters in Dubai. I remember coming back from one such meeting and had only just walked in the front door and put my cases down when the phone rang and within a couple of hours I was back at Heathrow, ready to fly to New Zealand because a colleague had been taken ill. I did this without complaint for 13 years. Because my children had got used to me not being around, they just carried on their normal lives. But it is a lot different if you have a young family. It can be a lonely business. I've worked with guys who have had a brilliant five days doing a Test and have called their partner feeling on top of the world and at the other end of the phone is the most miserable person in the world, because they've had to deal with all the domestic shit on their own. It happened to me as well, but not as often and only when my brother Barrie was seriously ill, and I'd call Jo and be told he'd taken a turn for the worse.

Barrie was 72 when he died in October 2014 and it hit me hard. As my oldest brother I looked up to him. He loved his sport – racing, football and cricket which he played to a decent standard as well. He was a hopeless gambler – worse than me which is saying something – but when we got together the time flew by. He was the only person I could talk to about any subject you care to mention and he always gave me good advice. Then suddenly he wasn't there. My younger brother Jeff is totally different to Barrie and myself. He is more calm and quiet and not the person I could unburden myself to when I had a few problems.

A few months after Barrie passed away I was in Australia to umpire in my third ICC World Cup early in 2015 and initially things went very well. I did a couple of warm-up games in New Zealand against Sri Lanka before the tournament and then stood in Adelaide for India versus Pakistan, which is always lively. Nine days later I was in Canberra for West Indies v Zimbabwe. There was a quick turnaround after that game and three days later I stood in Sydney where South Africa thrashed West Indies by 257 runs thanks to a fantastic 162 not out by AB de Villiers and five wickets for Imran Tahir. My next game wasn't until 8 March, also in Sydney, so I had a bit of downtime to look forward to.

Jeff Crowe was with us as one of the match referees and the following day – a Saturday – he flew back to New Zealand to spend some time with his brother Martin. I'd played against and also coached Martin back in the 1980s and I wanted to go with Jeff to see him. Martin had been diagnosed with cancer in 2012, been given the all-clear and then been told the illness had returned in 2014. Jeff was happy to have some company, but the ICC weren't keen that their umpires started flying off here and there in the middle of their marquee tournament so I stayed in Australia. Before he left, Jeff told myself, Aleem Dar, Richard Illingworth and Michael Gough – who would be the umpiring team for the match – to start our preparations on Friday 6 March, two days before the game. We arranged a time to meet at the hotel on that day before travelling to the ground. Jeff also asked us to check in every night with our security officer, a former soldier called Richard Alexander who was a lovely guy and looked out for us.

So, the best part of a week off in Sydney, one of my favourite cities. What's not to like? I had nothing in my diary, so I turned off my laptop. As far as I was concerned, I was off duty for the next few days. Now, the first thing I did when I arrived in any hotel anywhere in the world was unplug the phone in the room. The only time I ever answered a hotel-room phone was when I went to India to umpire for the first time in 2007 and a bookmaker at the other end of the line, who spoke very good English, offered me all sorts of inducements ahead of a one-day international against Pakistan. I reported this to ICC but vowed after that day never to pick up a hotel phone. Anyway, anyone who needed to get hold of me had my mobile number if there was an emergency.

The only stipulation was checking in with Richard every evening so I got into a bit of a routine, meeting him for a drink in a bar close to Sydney Harbour Bridge we both knew just before 7pm, after the ferry had docked. I spent some time in Manly meeting old friends and had a very convivial afternoon in Watson's Bay with the Parkinsons – Michael, or Sir Michael as I always call him even though he hates it, and his wife Mary – who I have known for many years. Parky gave me some sound advice about being in the public eye when I became an international umpire and he helped me out a couple of times with fundraising when I was chairman of Slough Cricket Club for a couple of years during a period when they moved to a new ground.

Anyway, we had a lovely lunch and, as usual, I made my way off the ferry to the bar early in the evening to meet Richard. As soon as I saw him, I knew something was wrong. He told me that I had missed a planned seminar with local umpires earlier that day which had been organised by Simon Taufel, who was now coaching and mentoring umpires for ICC having been a top official himself of course.

As an umpire, Simon was the best I ever worked with. His decision-making was outstanding – he was streets ahead of the rest of us in that regard. But, unlike me, I felt he wasn't a people person. He was completely dedicated to cricket and it was all he wanted to talk about – again, unlike me. On the field we got along fine, but I always found him a bit condescending towards me. It was his way or no way and I wasn't a great fan of that attitude. But professionally, we never had any issues. You can't get on famously with everyone in life.

Now me missing a seminar with the local umpires in Sydney was, on the face of it, no big deal. Simon and Aleem did the talk and after speaking to Richard I thought no more about it. True, I hadn't been around the hotel much during those few days. I would get up early, go for one of my five- or six-mile constitutionals to get a good sweat on, come back to shower and change and be off out again within a few minutes. But no one had told me I had to be at the seminar. No one had called me on my mobile to remind me and there were enough people who had my number.

The following day I had an email from Vince van der Bijl, the ICC's umpires' and referees' manager. Simon had written to him and the suggestion was that I had been insubordinate for missing the seminar and not spending enough time in the hotel. I took massive offence to the use of the word insubordination, and when Jeff returned from New Zealand he blew his stack as well. As far as he was concerned, I'd broken no rules. I'd checked in with Richard every night and I was ready to go back to work on the Friday before Australia versus Sri Lanka as arranged. I felt for Jeff, who flew into this shitstorm having just visited his dying brother. If I say I will do something, I will always honour that commitment and I had already taken part in a few of these seminars during the World Cup. I wanted to offer advice to the next generation of umpires, I was happy to give something back.

Fortunately, Denis Burns, my coach, and his wife Margaret flew into Sydney before the game because, without his calming influence, I would have walked out on the tournament there and then and been happy to tell the world the reasons why, even if it meant my career as an elite umpire would be over. Denis calmed me down and got me through the Australia–Sri Lanka game. That was also my 100th one-day international as an umpire and Simon had arranged for the other guys working with me to sign one of the stumps. He handed it over to me at the end of the game without a lot of ceremony because he knew how I was pissed off with him to put it mildly.

To this day I don't know how I didn't shove the stump up his backside. He seemed impervious to the distress he'd caused. Basically, Jeff, Richard and I had been accused of concocting a story and we weren't to be believed. The funny thing is that four years later, when I umpired for the last time at the Sydney Cricket Ground, the stump was still in the corner of the changing room and is probably there now.

I was still fuming when I flew on to Hobart to do Australia versus Scotland. Denis was there to babysit me and gradually I calmed down. I did another game in Melbourne and the semi-final between New Zealand and South Africa in Auckland before flying home. Jeff was as angry about what had happened as I was and, shortly after the tournament finished, he stopped off in Dubai on his way to another series to offer his resignation to Vince van der Bijl. If it had been accepted I would have resigned as well, no question. But by then Vince was beginning to regret his decision to send that email without talking to either Jeff, Richard or myself first to get an explanation. He talked Jeff out of quitting but for the next year or so I wanted nothing to do with Taufel. If I knew he was working around the same series as me I would make sure Denis told him to stay clear.

Even when I'd had a bad day at work, I didn't dwell on it too long. When I pulled back the curtains the next morning it was like a fresh start for me. I can reboot and start again quite easily but this incident took a lot of time to get over. I couldn't get over the fact that someone I had respected had accused me of insubordination. I carried on my work and for the next 18 months or so I stood in series all over the world – Sri Lanka, India, Australia, West Indies, South Africa and New Zealand. Even by my standards it was a very hectic schedule and, for the first time since I started umpiring, I began to feel tired. DRS had come in as well which put extra demands on umpires and while I still loved the job I didn't quite drive to the airport with the same enthusiasm as before.

The first inkling I had that something was wrong with me came in February 2016 when I came back from New Zealand where I'd stood in a one-day series against Australia. Since I'd started umpiring, my routine, as soon as I'd stepped back into the house and given everyone a hug, was to take my passport out of my pocket and place it along with any foreign currency in a bag on top of the fridge in the kitchen. George was there along with Jo and still reminds me to this day what I did with my passport instead of putting it in my bag. I opened the fridge door and very deliberately placed it between some slices of cheese and ham. What was all that about?

Three years on I now realise that I was having a breakdown. Was I tired? Very much so. Was I depressed? That's a strong term but I probably was. Did I do anything about it? Did I talk to anyone? Of course not. I didn't feel I could turn to anyone anyway, now that Barrie had gone. So I bottled it all up, tried to shut everything out and over the next few weeks retreated into myself. How Jo and the kids put up with me during that time I'll never know because I was horrible to be around. I started to hit the booze. There would be a couple of lagers to get me going then one or sometimes two bottles of wine – a day.

When I did go out, I was heavily disguised again and if I spotted someone I knew I'd dive into the nearest shop until they had passed by. I must have spent hours in the various charity shops along the streets in Hove. I didn't want to see anyone and I didn't want to do anything. My daily routine consisted of sitting in my armchair, shuffling outside occasionally from sheer boredom, and getting slowly arse-holed. It got so bad and I felt so low that I wasn't even watching racing on TV and only having the very occasional flutter.

Once again, as he'd done in Sydney, Denis Burns was my knight in shining armour. Every year the umpires assemble in Dubai for a catch-up and the night before we all meet in a bar for a few drinks and a reunion. It's the only time of the year when we are all in the same room together and once again it was a very convivial evening – Denis having persuaded me to make the trip when I didn't feel like it. I'm glad I did. That night I went outside for a cigarette with Denis and for the next hour or so I unburdened myself to him. The conversation I should have had a year or so earlier finally took place as I told him how I felt. Burnout, depression – probably a mix of both – had brought me to the point where I needed to take a proper break from the game, whether it lasted a few weeks or a few months. I could not go on the way I felt.

We agreed to meet again the next day after the first session of the seminar. Denis and I went to see my ICC line manager Adrian Griffiths in his office and told him I needed to take time out. I didn't go into all the details and it certainly came as a surprise to him, but he agreed without hesitation and told me to have as much time as I wanted away from the game. It was wonderful that ICC were being so understanding, less so a few days later when I got an email telling me I would only get my basic salary while I was not working. Money has never motivated me. As long as I've got enough for a pint and a packet of fags, I'm fine. But I thought that was a bit callous.

But ICC were supportive and so was Chris Kelly, the England and Wales Cricket Board (ECB)'s umpires' manager. Chris would call me twice a week to see how I was, and I also got in touch with the sports psychologist Michael Caulfield, who I have known since he did some work at Sussex many years ago. Michael has also worked for the Jockey Club and with Gareth Southgate, the England football manager, when he was in charge of Middlesbrough. Michael told me to go and buy a book written by

Alastair Campbell, Tony Blair's spin doctor when he was prime minister, called *The Happy Depressive*. I must have read it about 20 times, and it really helped. Michael would call every other day and so did Denis. Looking back on what happened now, I find it quite humbling that they were prepared to help and support me in the way they did. I did start to feel a little better, but I still saw myself as some little prick who'd had a moment in his life he couldn't handle. Gradually though, with their help and, of course, the love and support of my family, I started to improve.

In the end I found a solution. Every day, come rain or shine, I would go for a three-hour walk whether I was in Windsor or Hove. I must have worn out about five pairs of trainers but it changed me. I lost weight, I cut back on the booze big time and rather than avoiding people I knew I would go up and start talking to total strangers. Denis rang me one day and said that I sounded totally different. I was looking forward again and I wanted to go back to work. Jo wasn't sure that I was ready, and insisted that if I started struggling again I had to come home straightaway, no matter where I was or what I was doing.

I returned to international umpiring in a Test match between West Indies and Australia in Jamaica. Mind you, I nearly didn't make it. When I got to the check-in desk at Heathrow before boarding the flight, I was horrified to discover that I'd brought Jo's passport instead of my own. Panic stations. But, as always, Jo played a blinder. She was nearly home when I called, and picked up my passport and was back at Heathrow in time for me to make the plane. It wasn't in the fridge either before you wonder.

The following year, and fully recovered, my schedule took me back to Zimbabwe, a country I have always enjoyed visiting over the years, despite the problems caused by the Mugabe regime. They love their cricket and the people are incredibly friendly and helpful. Because of my experience, ICC had started to put me together with umpires who were still relatively new. It's rewarding to see them succeeding, often in very challenging circumstances, as an incident when we arrived in Harare illustrated.

I travelled out with Denis Burns and match referee Richie Richardson. It was a big series – India were there for three one-day internationals and three T20s. All the games were sold out and, as usual, there was lots of publicity surrounding the Indian team.

We arranged to meet the Zimbabwe umpires, Russell Tiffin, Jeremiah Matibiri and Iknow Chabi, at the Harare Sports Club. Just before we sat down I got Denis's attention.

'Who's that geezer? Haven't seen him before.'

Denis: 'Iknow.'

'I know you know, but I don't bloody know! That's why I'm asking you.'

Denis: 'That's what I'm telling you, Iknow.'

'What am I supposed to call the geezer if you won't tell me what his bloody name is?'

Denis: 'His name is Iknow.'

'You're having a laugh.'

Denis: 'His name is Iknow Chabi.'

'Stroll on. Alright! Hello chubby Chabi!'

We were upbeat and positive and I was looking forward to working with Iknow and the others. It was also Richie's first series as an ICC match referee, and he gave a short speech on how he was looking forward to a great team display from everyone. Then the local umpires broke the news to us. 'We haven't been paid for six months. If Zimbabwe Cricket do not pay us what they owe us by close of business tomorrow we will not umpire in this series.' Shit, this is serious. You could have heard a pin drop.

I sat down with Richie and Denis at the Rainbow Towers Hotel. The financial issues were somebody else's problem – ICC or Zimbabwe Cricket. I just wanted to support the umpires and get them focused for the games. Denis and Richie contacted the ICC and the Zimbabwe authorities and asked for an emergency meeting. I contacted the umpires and arranged some third-umpire simulations for the following day. The situation was messy, but fortunately it was sorted out before the first game. With India in town, Zimbabwe's board had too much to lose financially if the series didn't go ahead but I didn't like that their umpires had been put in such a difficult position. If they'd have gone on strike I would have supported them.

Zimbabwe is a great country but the infrastructure back then was not great. Like the Indian team, we spent one night in the Rainbow Towers and then insisted that we be relocated into a more comfortable place. The lifts weren't working and on the previous day the restaurant had bread, but no butter. On the morning we left the restaurant had butter, but no bread!

I'd also had an interesting encounter late one evening. I had been given a room on the 16th floor. Every other room on this floor had been booked for the deputy president who was staying there with most of his ministers. The hotel is notorious for 'ladies of the night' who were quite brazen in approaching you. I was fast asleep when there was a knock at my door around midnight. A scantily clad young lady smiled as she stood in the doorway.

'I have been sent for the minister.'

'Do I look like a bloody minister?'

I was back in Zimbabwe again a few months later for a series against Sri Lanka with Australia's Simon Fry. One night I got back to the hotel and couldn't find my bag. I asked hotel security to search the room, I got Simon to search my room and I even asked the match referee Chris Broad to search my room, but it wasn't there. The bag contained my passport and my credit cards and money. It was the last thing I needed after the previous few months but fortunately a mate who knew someone in the local police force got to work.

The next morning the bag reappeared, with all the contents still there. Unfortunately, Simon, being the sensible chap that he is, had already cancelled all my cards for me and had to lend me a few dollars to tide me over. I laughed about it once the bag had miraculously reappeared but if it had happened a few months earlier I know my reaction would have been totally different. I took it as another sign that I was feeling better about myself.

When I was at my lowest ebb I never felt suicidal. It was more self-loathing, especially at the amount of drink I was pouring down my throat. But for a time I didn't really know who I was or where I was. I felt like a shell of a man. I didn't feel I could confide in anyone until that night in Dubai with Denis but looking back I should have seen the signs. After ten years on the treadmill I needed to get off. I was burnt out. I do wonder how I carried on working for as long as I did after the incident in Sydney with Simon Taufel. Even now, what happened still annoys me.

I know for sure that some of my former colleagues have experienced similar issues. But, like me, they cover it up for the main reason that it's a great life that you are loath to give up. Do the ICC have a duty to provide more pastoral care for umpires and referees? Perhaps. But maybe a better idea is to have people around you who can recognise the signs. I certainly wouldn't want anyone to experience what I did during those long months in 2016. In the end ten years of constant matches, meetings and travel wore me down to the point of collapse.

I appreciate it's the same for players, but they do get the physical release from training and I believe that makes a big difference, although it can be hard for players to unwind now. They are constantly in the spotlight, even more so since the advent of social media and camera phones. Looking back to when I played, there were always players who suffered from loneliness and depression. Cricket has a history of suicides among players. Tours back then were often three or four months long and if you weren't playing much it was even harder. I am certainly glad that I played when I did and I'm proud of the fact that I made the utmost of the talent I had – and enjoyed myself to the full off the field.

6

Gunner of the Gunners

IT depends on how old you are, but if someone mentions Slough one of two things will probably come to mind. John Betjeman's famous poem about the place, written in 1937, which begins 'Come friendly bombs and fall on Slough!' or the brilliant BBC sitcom written by Ricky Gervais and Stephen Merchant called *The Office*, which was set in the town. I never finished the poem but even now, when I'm watching one of the old episodes of *The Office* again and the 'Slough Trading Estate' sign comes up in the opening credits, I smile. When I was growing up in the 1960s and early 1970s the Slough Trading Estate was regarded as the last place you wanted to end up.

But I am proud to say I was born in Slough – on 19 August 1957, appropriately considering how my life has turned out, during the cricket season. I was the youngest of four: Maureen, Barrie, Jeff and me. There is a big age difference between us. Maureen was 42 when she passed away because of cancer in 1983 and Barrie was born in 1944. Mum Doreen and dad George were both Welsh. They came from a village called Ammanford in the far west of the country and, like quite a lot of Welsh people, they moved to Slough in the 1950s to escape from the coal mines and try to build a better life for them and their children. A lot of them ended up working for a Slough-based company called Coopers, who manufactured mechanical joints. Dad, who had been a miner himself, worked at Coopers quite happily for 15 years before deciding to try to build his own business. At the time we thought he was crazy, but he ended up being very successful.

He moved into a factory in Maidenhead and built a company hardening and softening metals. Dad was never idle. He hated not having something to do and he was a grafter. I definitely take after him in that regard. The business became very successful, so much so that we were able to leave our council house to live in a bungalow in a village called Cippenham, a few miles outside Slough, which is where I grew up. Physically, my father was an imposing figure. He was 6ft 4in but the thing I remember most about him, because I often felt the back of them when I stepped out of line as a kid, were his massive hands.

I inherited mum's genes – she was 5ft 4in. She worked on the production line in a biscuit factory and then helped out as a school cook. I remember her trudging home, carrying these vast pots of custard from the school kitchen which the kids had turned their noses up at, heating them up and serving them to me and Jeff to try to build us up. Mum and dad got on well, but they'd occasionally have these massive arguments – usually on a Sunday afternoon for some reason – which would be conducted almost entirely in Welsh, with the odd English expletive thrown in for effect.

Despite the age difference I spent a lot of time with Maureen. She was a bright and intelligent girl who went to Slough High School, which was quite posh in those days. She left school at 18 and worked her way up in the local NatWest bank. Funnily enough, the manager at the branch she worked in was Dick Holste, who was later my benefit treasurer when I played for Sussex and was on the committee at Hove for many years.

She married a football-mad Geordie called Jimmy Eyres who played until he was 60 and they had two fantastic kids, Phillip and Jo, who I still see regularly. I have fond memories of Maureen. When she died, my cricket career was on the crest of a wave. I'd come down to Sussex from Middlesex and had been picked by England for the Ashes tour down under in 1982/83 and the World Cup a few months later. I was in Australia when I got a phone call to say Maureen had been diagnosed with cancer. I wanted to come home straightaway, but Maureen insisted I stayed out there as did mum and dad. She survived until I got home but died shortly afterwards. Even now, nearly 40 years later, I still miss my big sister very much.

If you had met all four of us together you wouldn't know Jeff was our brother. He's so quiet and unassuming, compared to his remaining siblings. Jeff always loved the countryside and in Cippenham we were surrounded by fields and farms. When he left school he immediately went to work on a farm, and he became a very good show jumper. He won a trophy at the Horse of the Year Show at Wembley, which was unheard of for a kid from Slough. While I went off to the village green to play football or cricket, he went to the farm and we'd meet up later in the day at the dinner table to exchange stories about our day and try to eat some of mum's custard. He wasn't games-minded like Barrie and me. When we went on holiday to Butlin's, Jeff would go to the beach to ride the ponies and I'd drive my dad insane all day by making him play table tennis, putting and cricket with me.

Jeff was a grafter too. I can still remember him coming home one Christmas with calluses all over his hands from where he'd been plucking turkeys on the farm all day. At least we got a nice Christmas dinner because of his efforts. I recall one day coming home from school and there was this massive 16-hand horse tethered up to a post in the back garden which Jeff had been breaking in for a local farmer! He then moved to Henley and worked for a family called the Bowdens and was still there into his 60s. He ended up breeding horses and breaking them in for people and did it very successfully.

Barrie was the other sportsman in our family and growing up I was in awe of him. He was 13 when I was born and had already gained a reputation locally for his football ability. He started out as a forward but it was in midfield where he caught the eye of one of the local Arsenal scouts. He played for the Gunners in their youth team and reserves for a bit and then Chelsea took him on. Tommy Docherty, who was the manager at Stamford Bridge at the time, scouted him in a reserve game and liked the look of him, so they signed him for a small fee. In those days, clubs could afford to carry squads of 40 or more pros and apprentices, mainly because they didn't pay much, the maximum wage having only been abolished in January 1961. I can't have been more than six or seven years old when Barrie took me to Stamford Bridge for the first time and I stood on the wide-open terraces, with the pitch still surrounded by a dog track, to watch him play a reserve-team game.

He was very talented – more so than me – but Barrie didn't have my commitment or dedication. He loved being the life and soul of any gathering, and he had the ability to make people laugh. He loved football and he loved cricket but his real passion, which he passed on to me, was horse racing and having a punt. I think it was one of Barrie's greatest regrets that he never played a game for Chelsea while a greyhounds meeting was in progress around the Stamford Bridge track. That would have been heaven for him.

His love of racing was to cost him his career at Chelsea when he turned up on the wrong day for a match having gone to a race meeting when he should have been playing for the reserves. In 1965 he moved to Peterborough United and it was there where he made his Football League debut. He had a couple of seasons with Peterborough and played 20-odd games and then had a trial at Bristol Rovers before dropping into what was still known then as the amateur game, even though players at the top level earned a decent living. Barrie had a good non-league career, starting at Worcester City and followed by spells with Gloucester City, Dover Athletic, Guildford and finally our local club Burnham, which 30-odd years later appointed me as their chairman. Of which more later.

With Barrie such a massive influence, it was natural that I would gravitate towards football above other sports in my formative years, even though I played a lot of cricket and even some rugby either at school or on the village green. Peter Osgood, who became a legendary striker for Chelsea, lived fairly close by in Windsor and was in the reserves at the same time as Barrie and he used to come to our house a lot. I would be kicking a ball around in the garden and 'Ossie' would be nagging me all the time to use both feet. He was a fantastic player. I know it's an old man's story, but if he was playing now he would score hundreds of goals, he was a natural finisher. But being around people like him drove me on. I wanted to be like Osgood. I wanted to be like Barrie.

Barrie wasn't afraid to stand up for himself. Peter Osgood used to tell a story of a game against Swansea when John Charles, one of the all-time greats of Welsh football, gave Ossie a hard time. Chelsea's coaches got stuck into Ossie, even though the game had finished 0-0, until 17-year-old Barrie had heard enough and gave the coaches both barrels himself. They remained in touch long after Barrie and Ossie's careers were over. Barrie eventually married Anne and they had two smashing children, Denise and Neil, who I still see regularly to laugh about what their dad used to get up to. My two boys have carried on the family football tradition. George plays for Windsor FC and Michael in Brighton for Mile Oak FC. I try to watch them when I can.

I was so lucky as the youngest, especially at a time when the family were relatively well off thanks to the success of dad's business. He had a few quid but all I ever wanted was a pair of football boots or a cricket bat which he happily bought for me. I was nine when

I played my first competitive game for Cippenham Cricket Club, batting at no.11 when someone didn't turn up. I made eight not out. After a couple of years I moved up to play for Slough CC, sometimes walking four or so miles there for net practice and games. But at that age football still held much the greater appeal for me. I was never out of the back garden, where I would learn – as Peter Osgood told me – to kick the ball with both feet – or on the green in Cippenham where we would play the boys from Burnham, which is the next village, at either football or cricket. The green was the hub of the village and I formed some enduring friendships playing games there. All the big companies in Slough had their own immaculately maintained sports grounds as well so there was never a shortage of places to play, rain or shine.

Dad had played a bit of rugby when he was younger, and he was desperate for one of us to play it at a decent standard as he wasn't a great football fan, preferring cricket given the choice. At school we played rugby and athletics which wasn't a great deal of good for the football-mad Ian Gould. My parents and siblings were very supportive, but it was our sports master – a guy called Terry Davies – who really nurtured my football and cricketing ambitions. I went to Westgate Secondary Modern School in Cippenham or 'Westgate Secondary Borstal' as we called it, and although I was okay at academic subjects I was always counting down the hours until I could be outside on the sports field.

Terry had run for Wales and played rugby for London Welsh, and he could see I had some talent and encouraged me in any sport I wanted to do. He would make sure I had time off lessons to play representative football or cricket and he'd often take me to the matches himself because my parents were still at work and didn't have a car in those days anyway.

So how did I end up being a goalkeeper? At that age I wasn't a lot different in height to most of the other boys and I just loved being involved as much as I could in the game. I was brave and agile – it certainly wasn't a case of the smallest having to go in goal. I wanted to be between the posts. I'd watch *Match of the Day* when it started in 1966 or later ITV's *The Big Match* on Sunday afternoons and my heroes were all goalkeepers like Tommy Lawrence at Liverpool, Gordon Banks of course and Ron Springett, who played for England even though he was only 5ft 7in.

I first played representative football for Slough Schools under-11s in the late 1960s and started to get noticed. I remember winning a Junior Sportsman of the Year trophy in a competition that was organised by the local paper which was a very big deal in those days. I still have the newspaper cutting showing me, and Jane Admans who won the girls' award, on the back page holding the trophy aloft in my right hand wearing a shirt with a massive winged collar. I sometimes wonder what happened to Jane.

I was in goal for Slough Schools' under-15s at the end of 1972 in a match at Slough Town's old stadium The Dolphin. I must have had a decent game because Slough Town's manager Tommy Lawrence approached me afterwards to invite me to train with Arsenal's juniors at the Gunners' training ground at London Colney. I'd already decided Arsenal was the team I would support. Everyone else in Cippenham followed Chelsea, Fulham, Brentford, QPR or Reading because they were the local-ish clubs but I was always a bit of a maverick. Slough was a big football town back then. Some major clubs were all within striking distance and players who didn't make it professionally would come back and play for Slough Town, nicknamed the Rebels, who were a good side and got to the old FA Amateur Cup Final at Wembley in 1973, the penultimate year before the competition was abolished. I was there to see them lose 1-0 to Walton & Hersham but they also won the Athenian League a couple of times at the start of the 1970s when they used to get crowds of 2,000 or more.

My trial game for Arsenal was a bit of an eye-opener. They must have lost their previous league match because the manager, Bertie Mee, played a full-strength side in a friendly at the training ground against London Universities. There was the 15-year-old me in goal behind a back four of Pat Rice, Sammy Nelson, Frank McLintock and Peter Simpson. I got there, changed quickly and kept my mouth shut but once the game had started I was fine. I absolutely loved it. I think the Arsenal XI won by five or six goals and with a back four of that experience in front of me I hardly had a save to make, but I thought I did okay.

After the game I went back to get changed but Bertie Mee had decided a 90-minute stroll against a team of students wasn't enough punishment for his players, so he made us run around London Colney for an hour. All the time I was an apprentice at Arsenal, the punishment for a bad result by the first team was the same: a game against a side they would beat easily to boost confidence and laps and laps of London Colney. Not very scientific, but it seemed to work.

In 1973 the school leaving age was raised by the government to 16, but provided the school's headmaster had given permission you were allowed to leave at 15 to take up an apprenticeship. The letter from Arsenal offering me mine arrived in May 1973. I would be paid £7 per week until August when it would go up to £8 a week. After my rise to £8 I took home £7.43 following deductions, but Arsenal did pay my train fare from Slough to London and gave my parents £20 towards my keep. Most of my £7.43 went to mum as well. Not that I minded. I had taken the first step towards becoming a professional footballer. I was absolutely loving life.

Walking into the marble entrance hall at Highbury – Arsenal's old stadium – to sign my apprenticeship is something I can remember as if it was yesterday. I had left school on the last day of term but because I wasn't due to report to the club for another six weeks I needed to find something to do. Mum got me a job at the Montrose Foundry in Cippenham, which was a real eye-opener for a wet-behind-the-ears 15-year-old. The heat of the furnace was indescribable. How anyone worked in those temperatures day after day was beyond me. It was hard, physical graft but it made me even more determined to follow a path in sport because working in a factory looked too much like hard work. Every night I'd come home, have my tea and then go out for a run, regardless of how tired I was. But the foundry work did toughen me up. I started to fill out a bit so by the time I began at Arsenal I felt physically able to cope.

And of course, goalkeepers in those days weren't expected to come through a crowd in the six-yard box to claim every corner or cross. That's what your centre-half did. Guys like Les Green at Derby County and Laurie Sivell of Ipswich Town were similar in stature to me but they played week-in week-out and won titles and trophies with their clubs. If you were agile and brave and knew your angles in the six-yard box you had a chance, even if you weren't that tall.

Anyway, I wasn't that much smaller than Arsenal's first choice Bob Wilson and his understudy Jeff Barnett, who were both brilliant goalkeepers. So size was never an issue when I started but within a couple of years it became so. Suddenly, defenders had to be a bit more than head-it-and-kick-it merchants.

They were expected to play out a bit, like Franz Beckenbauer did so successfully for West Germany when they won the World Cup in 1974. On the continent, goalkeepers began playing like sweepers and soon some of those ideas started to creep into the English game as well. And the ball began to get lighter too, so it was easier to knock it into the box. When I started, we still played with a traditional leather ball. When I finished, the lightweight panelled football initially made famous by Adidas in the mid-70s was all the rage.

My first reserve-team game was at Fulham in 1973 when I was 16. In the Football Combination reserve league we either played on Wednesday or Saturday afternoon and that day at Craven Cottage I had a stormer. We won 1-0 and everything that came my way I saved. I caught every cross and stopped every shot. Our manager Ian Crawford, who also looked after the youth team, collared me after the game and put his arm around me. 'That was unbelievable,' he said. Then, as I was leaving the dressing room, Fulham manager Alec Stock, who was a bit of a legendary figure in the game at the time, spoke to me and was full of praise, before warning me: 'You've got to keep working hard.'

Similarly, I remember a youth-team game against Tottenham who had Glenn Hoddle playing for them. After a few minutes I noticed an elderly chap standing by the goalpost and recognised him as Bill Nicholson, who had led Spurs to the league and cup double in the 1960s. I assumed he'd come to watch Hoddle, but I had another blinder. He caught me up as I was walking back to the dressing room. 'Well played lad, but don't stop working hard,' were his words. I knew I was doing okay, and because people like Alec Stock and Bill Nicholson had praised me I really felt my football career was only going one way but, the truth is, I never got close to the first team at Arsenal.

Bob Wilson was hardly ever injured and when he was, Jeff Barnett came in. Jeff played in the 1972 FA Cup Final when Arsenal lost 1-0 to Leeds United and he started next season, but Bob was back when he recovered from injury.

It was becoming a more physical game as well. I remember one reserve-team match I played for Arsenal at Stamford Bridge against Chelsea when I was 17. Brian Basson took a corner for Chelsea and Mickey Droy – a no-nonsense central defender who took no prisoners – attacked it as I was coming to claim the ball and Mickey almost bulldozed me into the back of the net. I ended up literally in the corner of the goal, fortunately with the ball still in my hands as the referee blew for a foul. That was probably the first time I thought my lack of stature might be an issue. Jimmy Rimmer came to Arsenal as Bob's eventual replacement and he looked massive compared to me, even though he was under 6ft. They also signed Neil Freeman who was 6ft 2in and he was enormous as well.

But it was still a great environment to be around and we had so much fun. Towards the end of my time guys like David O'Leary, Frank Stapleton and Liam Brady had started to arrive from Ireland and there was also David Price, who was England Schoolboys captain as well and some player.

At Tottenham they had Hoddle and Neil McNab and at Chelsea Ray Wilkins. I remember playing in a schools' match for Slough against Hillingdon, which is where Ray was from, and I'd never seen anything like it. He was so talented – every pass and every touch came off. Liam Brady was the same. He was physically slight, but you could never knock him off the ball, it was like it was glued to his feet. Frank Stapleton worked his boots off, he would practice for hours after training had finished, and was very brave. I still see

Liam occasionally as he lives a couple of streets from me in Hove. We have a beer or two now and then and occasionally chat about the old days, although he always prefers to talk about something else other than football.

As apprentices we did the things expected of us back then like cleaning boots and sweeping the vast Highbury terraces or collecting litter from under the seats. It was basically a form of slave labour and the coach, Ian Crawford, was a hard taskmaster. One Saturday in December 1974 we won an important youth-team game in the morning and arranged to go out as a squad in the evening for Christmas in central London. The normal routine was that a few of us had to go to Highbury in the afternoon after playing in the morning to clean the changing rooms and hose down the showers after the first-team game. But because we were all going out, instead of four of us, we all decided to go to the ground so we could get it done quicker. We watched the game – a terrible 0-0 draw in front of around 20,000 supporters – and headed down to the changing rooms where eventually the players started trooping out. All except Leicester's Frank Worthington, Peter Shilton and Alan Birchenall, who were still in there gone six o'clock.

They must have been heading into London on a night out as well because they were drying their hair and preening themselves for ages. It was 6.15pm when Johnny Davies, one of the youth team lads, walked into their dressing room and bold as brass told Frank that 'if they haven't fucked off within five minutes, they'll be hosed down as well as the floor'. I saw Frank at a dinner many years later and he still remembered this cocky kid telling him to hurry up, pointing the hose in his direction with his hand hovering over the cold tap. The Leicester lads took the hint and we finished cleaning up in about ten minutes, but word of our escapade got back to Ian Crawford and, on the Monday morning, he made us run up and down the North Bank at Highbury for hours carrying a team-mate on our back. We were also fined a couple of quid and forced to take a cold bath in pairs. We were all pissed off – especially at the fine – but you had to take your punishment.

My biggest problem was timekeeping. Slough to London Colney these days is an easy car journey around the M25 but there was no motorway back then and hardly anyone I knew had a car, so I'd get the train to North London and we would be picked up at either Highbury, Southgate or Cockfosters and then taken to the training ground. I remember Ian having such a go at me about my timekeeping one day that I decided to make a point by walking home – without realising it was 35 miles. I think I made it as far as the bus stop a couple of miles down the road when it started to rain, got a bus to Watford and rang a mate of mine at work who picked me up hours later.

Surprisingly perhaps, there wasn't much of a hierarchy at Arsenal in those days. On days off we'd all be invited by the first-team players to have a drink with them. The usual haunt on a Saturday after a home game was a pub in Southgate called the White Hart and after a few pints in there we'd all troop down to the Coolbury Club in Tottenham, where the owner's interpretation of opening and closing hours was very liberal indeed. And you would fall into conversation with any of the so-called superstars quite easily. They liked cricket too. We used to play Spurs at Finsbury Park every summer and there would be thousands of people watching. I think I got a duck in my only appearance.

Arsenal were not a great side in those days. Bertie Mee's priority was to not concede goals so there were a lot of draws or scrappy 1-0 or 2-0 wins. Crowds weren't great either. By the end of that 1974/75 season a couple of the home games were watched by fewer than 18,000 people. Personally, I don't think that dour philosophy really changed at Arsenal until Arsene Wenger came along as manager, even though they did have some success under George Graham. By which time, of course, I was long gone.

In 1974, in a game at Luton Town, I injured my knee, which needed surgery. By then I had started to take cricket more seriously and when I was called into Bertie Mee's office at the end of the season it soon became evident he'd done his homework on me. He had spoken to one or two people at Middlesex, who were aware of me, and knew that cricket was something I could fall back on. He then told me very politely that I wouldn't be offered a professional contract. He was honest, which I appreciated, and it probably did me a favour because by then my yearning to become a footballer had been replaced by a desire to play professional cricket. And that was that. After seeing Bertie I went into the boot room and a lovely guy called Alf Fields, who looked after the players' equipment, handed me two sets of boots, my shin pads and gloves. I walked down to the Arsenal tube station and went straight to Lord's to practise with Middlesex's age-group teams.

It was only many years later that I realised I was the last of Arsenal's footballer-cricketers, following such greats such as Denis and Leslie Compton and Arthur Milton. I was lucky. Lots of lads from that era who were released by professional clubs saw football as their only chance of avoiding places like the Slough Trading Estate. Being rejected was a lot tougher for them. So that was the end of my Arsenal career – or so I thought. The following season they had a goalkeeping crisis and I played in an FA Youth Cup tie aged 18 against Ipswich Town at Portman Road and had a stormer. Afterwards, I fleetingly thought I had been too hasty in discarding a career in football. But the feeling soon passed. I hadn't had any sort of proper growth spurt and in that dressing room that night I was the smallest person by a few inches.

During the winter of 1975/76 I tried to rekindle my enthusiasm for football by signing for Slough Town, where a lot of mates from home were playing. I didn't keep goal for fear of getting an injury which would jeopardise my cricket and if I'm honest I didn't really enjoy it. I saw it as a way of keeping fit in the winter and earning a few quid to spend in the pub. We'd play in the afternoon, spend some of our wages in the pub next to the ground and the rest at the local dog track in the evening.

But Slough went from strength to strength. They won promotion to what is now the National League with a squad full of local players in the 1980s before falling on hard times when they sold their old ground at Wexham Park. They ended up ground-sharing with Windsor & Eton for a while but they are back in the town now playing in National League South. I still go and watch them occasionally. The ties that bind I suppose.

It wasn't until I moved to Sussex that I fell back in love with playing football again. I had a few games for Whitehawk, Shoreham and Lancing in what was the old Sussex County League. You'd be paid a few quid, which you'd be expected to put back over the bar after the game, the standard was decent and I enjoyed it a lot. I ran around in midfield and trained a couple of times a week so it was a good way of keeping the pounds off during the off-season. My oldest son Michael still plays at that level for a club called Mile Oak, and I go and watch him now and again.

When I started my grass-cutting business one of my contracts was with Burnham FC, just down the road from Cippenham. In 2009 the chairman,

Malcolm Higton, became ill and I was persuaded
by his wife Carol to take on his role. They were big
boots to fill because Malcolm had played for the club,
managed them and then become chairman. At the
time they were in the Southern League but Burnham
is essentially a village and crowds were never more
than about 50. They relied on a few people to put some
money in to pay the players, but they were punching
above their weight at that level. But both Barrie and I
had played there, and we regarded it as 'our' local club
so I felt a nostalgic pull towards the place.

One thing I refused to do was put my own
money in. I bought the odd round when the team won
and I was 100 per cent committed to the job. I raised
Burnham's profile, persuaded some local businesses to
sponsor the club and got more people using the bar
both on matchdays and during the week. In that first
season we did really well. I was umpiring on the day
we played Poole Town in a play-off and I heard we'd
lost – I was delighted because promotion would have
meant recruiting better players and the club simply
could not afford to do that. I had to give up after a
couple of years when my international umpiring career
took off and I couldn't guarantee to be in the country
for any length of time during the winter. Luckily,

Malcolm recovered and these days he is Burnham's president and the club are in the Hellenic League Premier Division, and doing pretty well at a new ground. I still look out for their results.

I'll always be a Gooner although, while I still go and watch Arsenal occasionally at the Emirates, I have developed a passion for watching non-league football in recent years. I enjoy plotting a Saturday afternoon out and travelling somewhere by train to take in a game. Last year I went to watch Slough at Havant & Waterlooville and caught up with Adrian Aymes, the former Hampshire wicketkeeper who I umpired many times and who was on Havant's coaching staff. I go and watch Whitehawk, who play in the Isthmian League, and Shoreham or Mile Oak in the Southern Combination League. I mind my own business, have a couple of beers in the clubhouse and go home.

Back in 1975, as my Arsenal career ended, I only had one thing on my mind – a career in cricket.

7

Middlesex Matters

I PROBABLY knew a few months before my meeting with Bertie Mee that I wouldn't be playing football for a living and, when I was 14, I started to take my cricket more seriously, even though football remained my first love. I'd moved from Cippenham to Slough Cricket Club and a chap there called Dave Collins got me a place on the Wrigley Foundation, a scheme set up in the early 1970s to encourage young cricketers. Dave also got me trials for the MCC Young Cricketers at the end of 1972 while I was still at Arsenal. With no reserve-team football over the Christmas holidays I would go to Finchley CC's indoor nets for practice with Middlesex. The facilities were fairly primitive, but at least they had indoor nets back then, unlike Lord's.

I was still 14 when I played my first second XI game – and it wasn't for Middlesex. Dave had some contacts at Kent, and they invited me to play in a Championship match against Essex at Dagenham at the end of July 1972, remarkably still a few weeks before my 15th birthday. Batting at no.7, I made three before becoming one of six victims for Keith Pont. We followed on after being bowled out for 80 but did a lot better in our second innings and I walked off with a red-inker – 13 not out – as the match was drawn. But Kent was a long way from Cippenham, and my parents were dead set against me moving there. If I was going to play for anyone it would be Middlesex.

Anyway, I did the trials and thought nothing more about it until I got a letter a few weeks later inviting me to join the MCC Young Cricketers. Dad was delighted, and certainly more pleased than when Arsenal had offered me an apprenticeship. If his youngest wasn't going to play rugby, then cricket was the next best thing in his eyes. The coaches were Len Muncer and Harry Sharp, who went on to score for Middlesex and remained a dear friend of mine for many years.

I was only there for a few months but it was a real eye-opener for a lad from Slough. I was the only player not attached to a county and it was a very competitive environment. I also had to quickly get used to how things were done at Lord's and it wasn't something I took to readily. I wasn't alone. One of my contemporaries was Ian Botham, and with Ian around there was always mischief to be had.

One of our jobs was to bowl at MCC members for a couple of hours every evening during the summer in the nets. I'd heard stories that members used to incentivise net bowlers to bowl them out by putting a coin on top of the stumps, but I couldn't believe that it still went on in 1973. The trick was to do your sessions with Ian, who hated it. He was as strong as an ox even then and would send down bouncer after bouncer. He wasn't interested in earning himself a few quid to put in the fruit machine of the Clarendon Court pub near the ground where we often went when we finished. He just wanted the sessions to be over as quickly as possible.

I think the longest we spent bowling at the members together was ten minutes. One tried to pull a bouncer and ended up being carried off to hospital for some emergency dental work. Even I bowled my very modest medium pace with a bit more venom when one of the egg-and-bacon tie brigade wandered over from the pavilion, took guard and balanced a 10p coin on the off stump. That's when they could get hold of us. Our changing room is where the Bowlers' Bar is at Lord's these days, and members would ring up requesting bowlers to come over to the Nursery Ground until one day someone yanked the phone out of its wall socket. No one at MCC noticed for months.

We were basically treated like servants. You grudgingly accepted having to sell scorecards and cushions to members and haul the covers on and off when it rained, but the members snapped their fingers and expected you to come running to the nets and bowl them a few half-volleys. So, before the Test match against West Indies we decided to have a little bit of fun. An hour or so prior to the start of play I was scurrying around the Long Room when I heard this piercing whistle and looked up to see Beefy beckoning me towards him. He handed me about ten packets of Wrigley's chewing gum and told me to chew as fast as I could. Ten minutes before the start of play, which back then was 11.30am, I spat out a big ball of gum and watched Ian surreptitiously attach it to the donger of the bell which Andy, the attendant, would shortly be ringing to signal five minutes until the start of play. We made our way to the front of the pavilion and watched the fun. Andy gave the thing four massive tugs but nothing happened – not a sound. On the fifth occasion he pulled so hard the rope fell off.

Unfortunately, someone had spotted us, and we were hauled in front of Jack Bailey, MCC's secretary. Jack had the right pedigree for the job, but he was a wonderful character who delighted in occasionally pricking the pomposity of the place. We got a ticking-off, nothing else. Years later, when Jack had retired to the press box to write match reports for *The Times*, he told me that after we'd left both he and his secretary had dissolved into fits of laughter.

Back then I was very much a batsman only. I'd kept a few times for Slough, but they had two very fine wicketkeepers already, so I wasn't going to push them out of the team. Roland Butcher was the wicketkeeper in the Young Cricketers, but my batting must have impressed Len and Harry because they recommended me to Don Bennett, the Middlesex coach, who was often working with the county's pros in adjacent nets to ours at Finchley. I'd made my debut for Middlesex seconds – ironically against Kent – at Dartford in 1973 and got a duck. I played five games in 1974 and made a half-century against Sussex at Hove and in 1975 I signed my first Middlesex contract on a yearly salary of £1,435 with £8.50 appearance money if I played in the County Championship or John Player Sunday League for the first team.

Entering that Middlesex dressing room for the first time was an ordeal. Mike Gatting signed at the same time as me and Gatt was from a similar background. Guys like Peter Parfitt, John Murray, John Price, Fred Titmus and Dennis Marriott were real old-school pros and they didn't treat us a lot better than the MCC members. It was totally different to Arsenal where the senior players thought of you as an equal. This was a lot more intimidating. We'd be at their beck and call – making tea, running errands for cigarettes or bits of equipment. You didn't mess with these guys but at the same time I was growing up fast. I resented it but we put up with it because Gatt and I both felt our careers were moving in the right direction. We were scoring second-team runs and once word got around that we could play a bit I think one or two of the older players felt their place might be under threat, hence the resentment we could feel towards us in those early months of our Middlesex careers.

To make us feel more a part of things, Don Bennett asked me to switch clubs and play for Brentham in the Middlesex League. I had a few games, but I didn't like it, not least because without a car it meant I wasn't getting home until late on a Saturday night. Eventually, Don allowed me to return to Slough. Don was a great coach. You had to work hard, and he was very demanding, especially if we'd had a bad day in the field. His post-match fielding drills were among the toughest I ever encountered, and I watched an awful lot of international cricketers being put through their paces. Don was a small bloke, but he was very strong and would smash balls at you to catch until your hands were sore. Forget that you might have to grip a bat the next day. It was almost like being in the Army. Don and Harry Sharp praised you very occasionally, so when they did it meant a lot.

Second-team cricket then was a very good standard and we played a lot of home games at Harrow Cricket Club, which was useful because it had almost as pronounced a slope as Lord's. I vividly remember a game at Lutterworth against Leicestershire in 1975 when Wayne Daniel, who was trying to qualify for county cricket, made his Middlesex debut, bowled like the wind and finished up with 12 wickets. I opened our batting with Graham Barlow and got 80 in the second innings. Gatt and his brother Steve – who went on to have an illustrious football career with Brighton &

Hove Albion among others – played, along with John Emburey and Wayne whom we quickly nicknamed 'Diamond'. The Leicestershire side included Nigel Briers, David Gower, Paddy Clift and Nick Cook.

A few days earlier Gatt had made his first-team debut in a Gillette Cup tie against Buckinghamshire and I was a bit miffed not to play as well, but the day after returning from Lutterworth I got a call from Don Bennett. John Murray's wife was in hospital and he wanted to be with her, so I was going to make my Championship debut against Nottinghamshire at Trent Bridge and keep wicket.

I still remember the shot I played to get my first runs in county cricket, a glide off the back foot which went past Bob White, with whom I later umpired when I joined the county circuit, to the boundary. The bowler was a lovely guy called Barry Stead, who died tragically young five years later. I made 25 and 33 in a drawn game. I didn't find it that much harder than second-team cricket, but I was involved in an incident that left me battered and bruised after a proper working-over from Clive Rice, the Nottinghamshire all-rounder.

I was keeping wicket and Clive had just gone past 50 when he rocked back and smashed a short ball from Norman Featherstone for four. The next thing I know Mike Smith was appealing to the square leg umpire Bill Alley because the bails were off and lying behind the stumps. Bill hadn't seen it – he was probably thinking about the little business he ran out of his car boot in those days selling golf balls. I certainly wasn't clever enough to have knocked the bails over so that they fell backwards but Clive was furious, calling me all sorts of names in Afrikaans, one of which was almost certainly 'fucking cheat'.

Not long after coming out to bat in our second innings Clive brought himself back on to bowl and let me have it. I remember hooking a bouncer one-handed for six during a 30-minute battering which left me with a lovely collection of bruises, much to the amusement of Tim Lamb, the non-striker at the other end. At the end of the game Clive was in slightly more conciliatory mood but he stopped short of apologising. 'Be careful,' he said, and left it at that. Later, when I joined the international umpires' panel, I saw Clive a few times in South Africa and he still didn't believe he'd hit his own wicket all those years ago.

A few weeks later at the end of July 1975 I was taught another valuable lesson – do what you are told – when I made my Sunday League debut against Yorkshire at Lord's. We scored 143/7 from our 40 overs – including a six off Chris Old in my 36. Back then that was regarded as a decent total. It took Yorkshire's openers John Hampshire and Geoff Boycott 37 overs to knock off the target including a generous donation of four overthrows by me. Patrolling in the covers – the only position in the field where I wasn't bored out of my mind – Hampshire called for a quick single and, as John Murray struggled to get up to the stumps shouting 'hold it, hold it', I threw in the ball, which missed the stumps by miles, and ended up in front of the pavilion with me trotting all the way after it as the senior pros tut-tutted their disapproval. A mistake by me, but an honest mistake, and I was not impressed with the attitude of some of my team-mates.

John retired at the end of the season. Nigel Ross was lined up to take his place, but he smashed his arm in a second-team game and by the start of the 1976 season I found myself first-choice wicketkeeper. It was a steep learning curve. I could catch the ball, I could dive and stop it but not a lot more and in those days the wickets at Lord's weren't great and by the middle of the long, hot summer of 76, they were turning square. Which was great for guys like Fred

Titmus and the emerging John Emburey and Phil Edmonds but not for the bloke floundering around behind the stumps. But I worked hard with Don Bennett to improve and the really good wicketkeepers on the circuit – guys like Alan Knott and Bob Taylor – were happy to pass on some tips when we faced Kent or Derbyshire. I was never going to be in the same class as wonderful players like that, but I watched and learned and gradually got better. And a few years later I would share an England dressing room with Bob.

The previous year Middlesex had got to both one-day finals and lost them, but a really good team was starting to emerge under captain Mike Brearley. Wayne Daniel was coming through, fast-medium bowler Allan Jones proved to be a brilliant signing from Somerset and as well as Gatt, Emburey and Edmonds we had players like Mike Selvey, Graham Barlow and Clive Radley. We went top of the Championship at the end of July and won the title against Surrey at the Oval on 2 September. A few hours earlier I had flown back from the Caribbean after touring the West Indies with Young England for the best part of six weeks.

I'm not sure if I regarded myself as one of the best young players in the country at the time but it was a wonderful experience, nonetheless. Among my team-mates were David Gower, Bill Athey, Gatt and Paul Downton – all of whom played for England – but there were also a few players who shouldn't have been anywhere near that squad and who I felt were picked because of their background – posh boys with an over-inflated sense of entitlement not matched by their ability. I probably did have a chip on my shoulder, but I resented that some of the players were only on that tour because they had the right connections at Lord's. We stayed in all sorts of places as we hopped from island to island and one abiding memory was facing a 16-year-old Malcolm Marshall when we played Barbados Schools in Bridgetown.

In 1977 we shared the County Championship title with Kent – only the third time that happened in the competition's history – with Gloucestershire a handful of points behind, and also won the Gillette Cup for the first time, beating Glamorgan by five wickets in a pretty one-sided final thanks to 85 by Clive Radley after we'd bowled very well to restrict them to 177/9 from 60 overs.

A year later we came third in the Championship, which was probably just as big an achievement as the previous two years. We won two more games and got 28 more points, but England call-ups hit us hard and we lost twice to Kent, who went on to win the title.

Only four players played in more games than me that year despite the most frightening experience I ever encountered on a cricket field. It was Friday, 26 May 1978 and we were chasing 166 on the final afternoon to beat Lancashire at Lord's. It would have been a lot less, but Wayne Daniel couldn't bowl in the second innings because of a hamstring injury and the pitch wasn't the best with length balls taking off by the third day. On that sort of pitch Colin Croft, leading Lancashire's attack, was as lethal as Diamond and I had just joined Gatt, who was batting superbly in the face of this onslaught, when Croft skulled me with a bouncer that hit me on the right temple.

If what happened subsequently had occurred today the injury lawyers would have made a small fortune on my compensation claim. As I lay prone on the pitch, having knocked over my stumps as I fell, our physio Johnny Miller was still trying to locate the wicket. Johnny's eyesight wasn't the best and he was partial to a whisky during the afternoon so Mike Brearley and some of the others literally had to guide him towards their stricken team-mate. There was no club doctor on site, so they had to appeal for a medic over the PA system. Then, when an ambulance was called to take me to Middlesex Hospital, I had to go on my own.

I remember coming around a couple of hours later when I was woken by the noise of the lady in the next bed being violently ill. My thigh pad was lying next to the bed and I still had my box on. I guess the doctors thought I'd just sleep it off. I got up, discharged myself and started walking down the road outside without a clue as to where I was going, or indeed where I was. Amazingly, a taxi driver who'd been at the game saw me staggering down the pavement in my whites and pulled over and drove me back to Lord's. Outside the Tavern pub, another Middlesex supporter grabbed me, led me into the bar and sat me down next to Jack Simmons and the Lancashire lads, who were having a quick pint before heading up to Headingley for their next game and apparently discussing whether I was dead or not!

Eventually Brian Reid, a guy I knew from Brentham Cricket Club, got hold of me and took me back to his house in Ealing. I had a blinding headache and was feeling dizzy not surprisingly, but it was still a couple of days before Middlesex organised for me to see a specialist, who told me to take a couple of weeks off. I had no X-ray or scan. Meanwhile, my mum and dad had gone to Torremolinos for their first ever foreign holiday and found out about what happened a couple of days after the incident when someone they had met in the hotel bar waved a copy of the *Daily Mail* in front of them on the beach with the headline 'Fury over Lord's bouncer victim' with a picture of me!

I must have looked a right state when I eventually got back to Slough. I was wearing Brian's clothes which would have been fine had he not been 6ft 5in tall and I had a massive bruise on the side of my head. Mum gave me dog's abuse before hugging me for about five minutes.

Earlier that year helmets had been used for the first time in World Series Cricket and Dennis Amiss, the England batsman, had designed his own rudimentary white one which looked more like a crash helmet. Demand was sky-high even though £29.95 was quite a bit of money in those days. They were very uncomfortable and took a lot of getting used to but by the end of that season most of the players on the circuit were wearing one. We were coming into an era when virtually all the counties had at least one outstanding fast bowler and I don't think it is any exaggeration to say that Dennis's invention probably saved lives.

It took me a long time to get used to facing fast bowling with confidence again even though I was back playing less than two weeks later when we took on Kent at Lord's. No concussion protocol in those days. Their opening pair were Kevin Jarvis, who was fast-medium at best, and Graham Dilley, considerably sharper and regarded then as a potential England player. Dill let me have a few bouncers and eventually I was caught behind, but not before I'd top-scored with 49 in our second innings. A few days later we played Warwickshire at Edgbaston when Bob Willis was trying to prove his fitness ahead of a Test match against Pakistan. We were 25/4 and then recovered slightly but when I came in after lunch Bob was into his second spell and charging in. My only scoring shot was a boundary punched off my nose and over the slips. Bob stood in front of me pissing himself with laughter before yorking me next ball. Prior to being hit by Croft, I'd played fast bowling well. I liked the challenge. I never bottled it after the incident, but I did struggle. And anyone who tells you they enjoy fast bowling is a liar. It's just that some batsmen play it better than others.

The Worcestershire attack in 1978 was led by another West Indian in Vanburn Holder, a colleague I was to have some fantastic times with when we later umpired together, but at New Road that July I made my only Middlesex century – 128 not out – when Keith Tomlins and I put on 209 for the sixth wicket. I should have scored more centuries and it's a regret from my playing days that I never made a hundred at Lord's. But having been capped in 1977, when I was still a teenager, I was regarded by then as a senior professional, although I was beginning to feel that my career was stagnating a bit despite the trophies we had won.

The 1979 season started off very wet. For one game against Sussex at the end of May we didn't bowl a ball. On days like that we used to train like lunatics in the morning then head up to Finchley Golf Club in the afternoon to hit a few balls or spend time in the bar. Play on the final day was called off early and, bored out of our minds, Graham Barlow dared me to try to hit a golf ball from the changing room on to the square at Lord's. Now, this was a challenge I couldn't resist, especially after the lads all lobbed a fiver into the pot if I managed it. As well as getting it between the veranda windows, there was the 4ft-high railing in front of the balcony to negotiate. All the lads asked was that I gave them enough notice to take cover when I hit the ball in case it ricocheted off the railing and back towards us.

The tee was the vast table in the changing room and Norman Featherstone suggested I use an upturned clothes brush to help get some elevation. Because of all the golf we'd played that spring I was hitting the ball quite nicely, but I have never struck a nine iron as well as I did that day, or since come to think of it. It sailed towards the target with the lads roaring their approval until we spotted Jack Bailey and head groundsman Jim Fairbrother walking towards the sodden square. The ball landed and plugged in the middle of the pitch earmarked for the World Cup Final a few weeks later. 'Great shot, Gunner,' shouted Mike Gatting as I frantically tried to hide my club. Too late. A few hours later I was hauled in front of Jack again. He thought it was one of the funniest things he'd ever seen but told me to grow up. Which was fair enough. A few hours later he joined us in the Tavern pub as we made a dent in the 60 quid I'd picked up.

Our performances that season were patchy. We came 14th in the Championship and lost in the semi-finals of the Gillette Cup to Somerset but I played regularly, although I didn't think I was necessarily improving that much as a player. Mike Brearley indulged me a bit and I liked him, to the extent that I even went around a few of the pubs in Kilburn collecting the bottles that punters would put their loose change in for his benefit until one day we turned up at a place run by an Irish guy who was a known sympathiser of the IRA. After collecting Mike's bottle, I proceeded to empty half of it into another which was being used to fund the cause of Irish republicanism.

In 1978 I had signed a three-year contract with the club but by the end of 1979 I'd had a gutful of Middlesex. Jack Bailey was trying to modernise Lord's, but Middlesex were treated like second-class citizens when we played there. I was going through the motions a bit and the relentless schedule in those days, when we thought nothing of driving from one end of the country to the next to start a three-day game the following day, was grinding me down. And I knew I hadn't fulfilled my potential. I was keeping wicket okay but there was no one putting me under pressure for my place. My closest friend in the dressing room was Clive Radley and as the 1979 season drifted towards its conclusion, which happened a lot in those days if you were out of contention to win a trophy, he suggested I go to New Zealand and play in the winter for Auckland. It was a big decision to cut my ties for four or five months, but I took the plunge and to this day I think it was one of the best moves I ever made in my playing career.

The New Zealand equivalent of the Championship was the Shell Shield, which had only started in 1975. There were only six teams so every game mattered. I loved the country from the moment I set foot in it. The scenery was stunning, the people friendly and the cricket competitive. On my debut at Eden Park, I top-scored with 54 when we drew with Wellington and that helped me settle in. My other scores in the competition didn't amount to much but I trained my nuts off and worked hard to improve my wicketkeeping when I played club cricket. It was a very enjoyable few months and when I came back for the start of the 1980 season, I felt rejuvenated and ready to move my career forward again.

It didn't take too long for my optimistic mood to be shattered. I turned up at the Barclays Sports Ground in Ealing at the end of March for day one of pre-season training and the first person I saw was Paul Downton, whom Middlesex had signed from

Kent during the winter. Being on the other side of the world I wasn't aware that Paul, one of the most promising wicketkeeper-batsmen in the country, was now a Middlesex player. And he wasn't coming to play in the second team.

First, Paul had to go off to Exeter University to finish his degree course so I started the season and played my part, for a while at least, in what was one of the most successful years in Middlesex's history. The county thought Wayne Daniel would be needed by West Indies for their tour of England and recruited Vince van der Bijl, a hulking South African quick bowler, as his replacement and someone I came across again when he worked for ICC years later.

But Diamond wasn't picked for the tour and that left us with a brilliant new-ball attack. They took 152 Championship wickets between them and it was a fantastic experience for me to keep wicket to two champion fast bowlers. We won the County Championship, finished third in the John Player League and beat Surrey in the final of the Gillette Cup. What turned out to be my last season with Middlesex was my most enjoyable.

But I wasn't scoring enough runs and I probably knew what was coming when Mike Brearley asked to have a chat before we were due to play Kent at Lord's at the end of July and told me that I was being left out and Paul was going to make his debut. Just as he told me, the skies darkened, and it pissed down for hours and they didn't play on the first day. I was disappointed of course, but when dad found out in the evening paper that I wasn't playing he was absolutely distraught. By then I was in the pub with my mates getting pissed and trying to figure out what to do next. A week later I played my last game for Middlesex, as a specialist batsman at no.5, and scored ten in a Sunday League match against Essex at Lord's before being caught off Keith Pont, the player who had dismissed me all those years ago when I played my first ever second-team game for Kent as a 14-year-old.

The club duly offered me a new contract but I knew I would never get regular cricket as a batsman in that Middlesex team. I wasn't good enough. Ironically, in mid-August I was chosen to play for Young England against the touring Australians at Worcester but by then I was back in the seconds and knew my future lay elsewhere.

But where? Earlier that summer we played Nottinghamshire in the Gillette Cup at Trent Bridge and Basharat Hassan, who batted in their top four, was keeping wicket for Notts. This surprised me, because Bruce French seemed to have established himself as wicketkeeper there and the word on the circuit was that he was a good 'un. A couple of the Notts lads spoke to me afterwards to see if I was interested but, flattered though I was, there was only one place I was going to end up.

Middlesex always enjoyed their trips to Hove. I remember going there for the first time with the seconds in 1974 and thinking how nice it was to play cricket a few hundred yards from the seaside. We used to stay in a hotel within walking distance so there was always an hour or two after play in either the Sussex Cricketer pub at the entrance or the squash club bar in the corner of the ground. As Middlesex got stronger in the 1970s, we could generally rely on beating Sussex with time to spare so we could enjoy a round of golf on the South Downs or just spend time on the beach. Our wives and girlfriends started to come along too and it was all very convivial.

Again, a few unofficial overtures were made. Sussex's wicketkeeper at the time was Arnold Long but he was coming to the end of his career and was struggling to cope with their two new fast bowlers Imran Khan and Garth Le Roux. But it wasn't until the end of October 1980 that Sussex formally approached me. I had a chat with Roy Stevens, the secretary, and I agreed to come down and meet the chairman, Tony Crole-Rees. I got off the train at Hove and it was a lovely, crisp autumnal morning. At that moment, before I'd even started to negotiate with Sussex, I knew this was where I wanted to be. I met Tony in the Sussex Cricketer pub and signed for £13,000 a year, the same money I'd been on at Middlesex.

A couple of hours later we went to Tony's flat on the seafront and he disappeared into the kitchen, came back and plonked a drink in front of me. 'I believe that's your favourite,' he said. 'I've done some research and I hear you like vodka and orange.' I never found out if that was the extent of Tony's 'research' into their new signing, but I had several vodka and oranges with him as afternoon turned into evening before heading back to London on the late train delighted to be a Sussex player.

8

Sussex by the Sea

W E WON two competitions during my nine years at Sussex, and it was one of the best moments of my career when I captained the county to the second of those in 1986, when we beat Lancashire to lift the NatWest Trophy. I'd taken over from John Barclay, who was struggling with a finger injury, earlier that summer and my permanent appointment as captain was ratified a few days after our victory at Lord's.

Although I had been John's vice-captain, I didn't covet the top job but there weren't many alternatives. Paul Parker was the only other candidate, but he was struggling a bit with form and fitness and didn't really recover either until he took over from me in 1988. So I felt obliged to do it but a few weeks into the 1987 season I knew I'd made a big mistake and by August I was so fed up I had to be talked into carrying on until the end of the season by Alan Wadey, who was chairman of the cricket committee. We only won seven games in all competitions and didn't win a Championship match at home all season.

But undoubtedly that Sussex team should have won more than two trophies during that era. Even when I was playing for Middlesex, there always seemed to be a youngster at Hove coming through when we played Sussex. To this day, I still say that Allan Green was the best young batsman I ever saw. I remember one game when he took on Wayne Daniel and Vincent van der Bijl with the composure and elegance of someone who'd played 50 Tests.

One of my biggest regrets when I eventually became captain was not doing enough to help Allan. I regard him as one of the greatest players to play for Sussex, he made it look so easy. If we'd had sports psychologists in those days they would have been able to try to help Allan but he simply fell out of love with the game and by 1989 he had retired. He was a very fine player though and on the way to the final in 1986 he played some wonderful innings.

Guys like Adrian Jones, Tony Pigott – the Harrow hurtler – and Dermot Reeve came through and we already had two fantastic overseas bowlers in Imran Khan and Garth Le Roux. At times it was a combustible mix. Every day I walked to the ground knowing it was either going to be a great laugh or someone would end up going for a team-mate's throat. But on the pitch we played hard and if we'd had a really good spin bowler, someone capable of running through a side in the right conditions, we'd have won two or three Championships. Chris Waller was very steady and could hold an end up, but he rarely ran through a team even on turning wickets.

And holding the thing together was John Barclay. John wasn't as good a player as Mike Brearley but as a captain he was definitely his equal. He understood what made people tick. He knew what to say and when to say it. I'd first come across him when I'd played for Slough against Eton College, where John was educated. We were a bit like the odd couple. The geezer from Slough and the public-school educated gent at wicketkeeper and first slip but we hit it off. John loved hearing what the lads had been up to the night before and the players would do anything for him. John could also bowl off spin and when him and

Chris Waller were bowling in tandem it wasn't much fun being close to the wicket. But Tim Booth-Jones would stand there for over after over, as someone like Zaheer Abbas lapped John and Chris for fun, without complaint, even if he came off at the end of the day covered in bruises.

John was a fine captain, a real thinker. He hated dull cricket. In that era of three-day matches it was usually up to the skippers to come up with an agreeable fourth-innings target on the last afternoon if there had been rain. John could be very persuasive. On more than one occasion he got much the better of the negotiations but was always the first to commiserate and buy a drink while his opposite number was still trying to work out how he'd been diddled by John.

In my first season in 1981 we should have won the Championship but ended up second by two points to Nottinghamshire. Two games that summer stick out. We played Kent at Tunbridge Wells in June and they batted really slowly in their first innings, only getting 250 in the 100th over. We had a first-innings lead of 51 and on the last afternoon Paul Parker and I bowled a few overs of full tosses and assorted dross to try to hasten the declaration. It left us needing 220 to win in what was effectively 25 overs.

By then I had started opening the batting in one-day cricket with Gehan Mendis, so John told us to go out and give it a go and we smashed 47 off the first five overs. If we'd continued at that rate we would have won but invariably wickets fell and in the final over Gehan was dismissed for 80 by Derek Underwood, who then took Chris Waller's wicket with the fourth ball, and we lost by 37 runs. John got a bit of stick from a few committee members that day but certainly not from the team.

Until Sussex finally won the Championship in 2003, the game their supporters talked about was what was effectively a title decider at Trent Bridge in early August 1981 when Nottinghamshire's last-wicket pair Eddie Hemmings and Mike Bore hung on for the last four overs in poor light to secure the draw. The incident which was always mentioned was Imran's leg-before appeal against Bore, which was turned down by the umpire Peter Stevens. My initial thought was that it was going down the leg side but I was the only member of our team who didn't think he was out. We finished the season by beating Yorkshire at Hove but Notts defeated Glamorgan and the title was theirs.

So a disappointing finish to my first season, but at the end of it I knew I'd made the right decision.

Things were going well away from cricket too. I'd first met Jo on a Sunday night in a pub called the Dumb Bell in Taplow and I fell for her straightaway. I'm not sure what she saw in me, but we started courting. She had a job as a receptionist with a firm called Varatio, a company my dad did a lot of business with. When she came to our house for the first time she got chatting to dad and he eventually realised that every time he called Varatio it was Jo he spoke to. They got on like a house on fire after that which made life a lot easier and by 1982 she had got herself a job in Brighton and moved down to Sussex.

Our flat was next to the Lansdowne pub in Hove which was run by Dave and Annette Day. Dave now owns a string of pubs in the Brighton area and they are still friends of ours. I used to get a lot of the boys to come down and eventually a few of the Brighton & Hove Albion footballers, who were in the old First Division and had reached the FA Cup Final in 1983, started frequenting it, including Steve Foster, who I still bump into these days for a drink now and again. There was also a guy called Chris Dittmar who became the world squash champion and used the squash courts at the cricket ground. It was 20 steps from my chair in the flat to my stool in the pub. Sussex were a very social team and county cricket back then was a very social game. But Jo and I also spent hours walking around Brighton and Hove, along the Sussex Downs or the coast. She loved the place and when I went back to Middlesex as coach a few years later I had to drag her out of Sussex. She was delighted when we were able to move back there when my umpiring career took off.

* * *

There are a lot of references in my story to horse racing. My passion for the sport goes back to when I was growing up, but it really developed after I joined Sussex.

As a kid, I remember taking my dad's bets to the local bookies. He always had a Yankee on Saturday and watched the ITV7 on *World of Sport* on Saturday afternoons. I don't remember going back too often to pick up any winnings, but he followed Newsboy, the tipster in the *Daily Mirror*, religiously.

Barrie loved racing as well and Jeff worked with horses for most of his life. It was the one thing the three of us had in common. There were a few racecourses close to where we lived – Windsor, Kempton Park and Newbury – and I can remember going to my first meeting with a bunch of mates at Newbury just for the craic. We didn't bet or study the horses much, but I soon began to fall in love with that environment.

There was a dog track around Slough Town's old football ground at the Dolphin and the Boxing Day meeting used to be a wonderful day out. Mum and dad's family would usually come up from Wales to spend Christmas with us and we would go there and enjoy ourselves. I quite liked dog racing but National Hunt jumping courses was where I wanted to be more than anything. It's almost an obsession now. If I have a day off, I try to go to a meeting somewhere. I love it.

What is it about a small racecourse that attracts me? Well mainly the people you meet there. I love the intimacy of places like my local track at Plumpton and the other smaller courses dotted around the country. No one bothers you and you meet all sorts of different people, who are all happy to have a chat and a drink. It's difficult to explain but National Hunt devotees will know what I mean. I remember going to Nottingham for the first time while I was playing at Trent Bridge many years ago and discovering to my horror that they were about to take down the hurdles and fences and concentrate on flat racing only a few weeks later. I was horrified and I haven't set foot in the place since.

Something similar happened at Windsor, which was my local track when I lived in Berkshire. The New Year's Day jumps meeting there used to be a spectacular afternoon out but these days they concentrate on flat racing, mainly on Monday nights in the summer. It's great for making money as it attracts a lot of people from the City but it's not so good for my bank balance. One of my friends had a 60th birthday party at one of their Monday meetings and the standard of the horses wasn't great to be honest. Yet I was charged £29 to get in and another £3 for a race card! It's not racing in my book either, just low-grade horses running from point A to the finish over any distance from six furlongs to a mile. Put it this way, I won't be putting any of my hard-earned back into Windsor's coffers for a while.

Where I live now in Hove, I can be at my local track Plumpton in 45 minutes. The train station is at the end of the course and the place is unrecognisable from when I first started going there when I came to Sussex in the early 1980s. It's my favourite course. They have improved the place so much in the last few years, and the facilities now for horses, trainers and punters are very good. The standard of racing isn't always the best, but the management understand that when they set the price you pay to get in. It's always well supported, particularly by the local trainers, and you never see an empty bar there. It can get a bit wet in the winter and that long uphill straight on a bleak January or February afternoon is not for the faint-hearted – put it this way, I wouldn't like to run around it, but I love the place. When I give up umpiring, I want to tick off the rest of the National Hunt tracks in the UK, places like Bangor-on-Dee and Ffos Las, which I have never been to.

Back in 1982 I remember having to go and play in a benefit game at Findon Cricket Club. It was on a Friday afternoon which I wasn't happy about as we had a rare weekend off and I was looking forward to spending it with Jo but it turned out to be one of the best decisions I ever made. That day I was fortunate to meet Josh Gifford, who trained his string of jumps horses at a yard a six hit away from the cricket ground in Findon Village.

The problem was that all Josh wanted to talk about was cricket, which he loved, and I wanted to talk about racing. In the end we compromised – we'd talk about each subject for an hour! But it was the start of a lifelong friendship which endured right up until 2012, when he passed away. By then he had been retired for ten years and his son Nick had taken over the yard and had become a great success in his own right with help from his sister Tina, a superb horsewoman who won three Olympic medals in eventing.

Josh was one of the humblest men I have ever met and his wife Althea gave him great support around the yard. He had so much fun even though training horses back then and now is a serious business. He could have between 80 and 100 horses in his yard at any one time and some seriously wealthy owners to deal with. I got to know him well and our friendship blossomed when he started inviting me to his yard to watch the horses working out on the gallops on the South Downs.

I would get up at 6am and be on the gallops by 7, in all weathers. Josh would point things out as the horses sped past and I enjoyed it so much I would sometimes go up there five or six times a week. I'd buy the *Sporting Life* and later the *Racing Post* religiously to study the form and see how Josh's horses were doing.

I met a lot of his owners and most of them, like Josh, were cricket nuts. During the summer Josh would take a few days off from the yard and tour the south-east with his racing mates playing cricket against clubs like the Hampshire Hogs and at wonderful grounds like Ascot Cricket Club, quite close to the racecourse there.

I always made every effort to go along because it was always such a fun few days. Some of the Sussex lads – Neil Lenham, Tony Pigott, Adrian Jones and Allan Green – used to come with me for the craic. It was a relaxing thing to do, spending time with a lot of interesting people and away from the pressures of the cricket environment. During the winter the Sussex boys who were still in England would regularly meet at Plumpton. Josh would invariably be there, and he'd introduce us to the other trainers and some of the jockeys, although in that company the conversation invariably turned to cricket. Sometimes, if Josh had a poor day and the owners were coming to the yard for an explanation as to why their horse had run badly, he would invite me over and I would spend time talking to them about cricket and having a laugh. Soon, their horse's performance would be forgotten about.

I played a few games of cricket with trainers and jockeys over the years and some of them were decent players. The former champion jockey Walter Swinburn and trainers Kim Bailey and Oliver Sherwood stood out although the jockeys were so worried about getting hit that, if the ball came towards them, they would get out of the way so as not to risk a broken bone.

I admired the discipline of the jockeys, virtually living on fresh air every day and risking life and limb every time they mounted a horse, especially the jump jockeys.

While my brother Jeff made a career working with horses, I sat on one only once. I'd had a few drinks at Josh's one lunchtime and he was walking out with a horse and invited me to jump on. I thought Josh had him on a short rein, but it was a bit longer than I expected and before I knew it this horse was galloping off with me hanging on for dear life. I'd rather have faced Malcolm Marshall and Wayne Daniel without a helmet on, it was that frightening.

It's a hard life being a trainer. Nick has had a lot of success like his dad and I still go over there, although not as often as I used to. I find it very relaxing just standing watching these magnificent animals being put through their paces.

I was fortunate to meet some great characters like Josh's stable jockeys Richard Rowe, a trainer in his own right now, and Declan Murphy, who never rode again after a terrible fall in 1994 at Ascot. Watching Declan and John Francome ride a horse was, for me, the equivalent of watching Viv Richards or Barry Richards bat.

Owning a horse never really interested me because I couldn't afford it but just after Josh had retired in 2002, Gerry Ryan, the former Brighton footballer, persuaded me to take a £500 share in a horse trained by Gerry Enright, who worked out of the old Lewes racecourse for many years before retiring in 2012. Fearless Fighter was being primed for a race at Plumpton until he broke his leg when he stepped down a rabbit hole and my £500 went down the hole with him.

By the time Josh retired, my umpiring career was taking off and over the years I have watched a lot of racing abroad in places like Melbourne, Mumbai and Cape Town. If we had a day off during a match and there was a racecourse nearby I would go. It was always a lot of fun, especially in India where their passion for racing is nearly as strong as it is for cricket. And you'd be surprised at the number of British jockeys and trainers you would bump into.

As for betting, I can hardly call myself a high-stakes gambler. I might have a few quid during one of the big festivals like Cheltenham but, when I go to places like Plumpton, I end up talking to so many different people that I often forget that a race is about to start and it's too late to bet. I'd much rather listen to Gary Moore, one of our top trainers in Sussex, than gamble anyway. I'll have a placepot or something, but the stakes will only be a couple of quid. I think the most I ever won was £340 and that was for an outlay of £2.70 on a four-horse accumulator who all came in. Anyone who tells me they are a consistent winner on National Hunt racing is being economical with the truth and I have certainly never chased my losses.

Even when I had the opportunity to make use of some inside information I missed out. I remember in the 1980s being told in the weighing room somewhere by Richard Rowe about a horse called River Lossie, who was a dead cert later that day at 11-2 in a race at Fontwell. Richard and I ended up going back into Findon for a drink and it was only when a group of race-goers came in ordering champagne, because River Lossie had romped home, that I remembered I should have put a bet on!

With all the other distractions available to cricketers these days I'm not sure there is the gambling culture in dressing rooms that there was when I played. Back then counties like Kent had a lot of serious punters in their team. Sussex less so, but I still remember an incident at Tunbridge Wells back in the 1980s.

A few days before, I'd played in a charity game with Walter Swinburn, and afterwards his driver tipped us off about a horse called Zilzal which was due to run at Goodwood while we were playing Kent in a Championship match. During the game and the daily journeys up and down the A26 to the ground all we talked about was how Zilzal was going to make us all rich. It became too much of a distraction if I'm honest. Our coach Stewart Storey was doing his nut, especially on the Friday – the last day of the match – when Zilzal was due to run.

Anyway, after a couple of declarations Kent set us 227 to win after lunch and we were going well at 105/2. A few minutes later, our 12th man Neil Lenham came running into the dressing room waving wads of tenners around 'Loadsamoney' style. Our collective £150 or so on the 2.50 at Goodwood had returned a very handsome profit. As the share-out began we suddenly started losing wickets and collapsed to 160/7. With fivers, tenners and kit all over the place, I couldn't find my thigh pad and improvised by stuffing as many notes as I could find down my trousers. Peter Moores, who briefly batted with me at the other end, found it hilarious, Stewart Storey less so. I didn't get many runs but thankfully Tony Pigott saw us home with an unbeaten half-century and we won by three wickets. A day I'll never forget – and racing continues to give me as much pleasure now as it did then.

* * *

Back in 1982 Sussex did turn potential into some silverware by winning the John Player League. We only lost one of our 16 games, winning 14 and setting a points record as well. A typical team would have me and Gehan opening, followed by Colin Wells, Paul Parker, Alan Wells, Garth Le Roux, Ian Greig, Paul Phillipson, Tony Pigott, John Barclay and Chris Waller. Even without Imran, who was captaining Pakistan that summer in England, that team covered all the bases in one-day cricket. We scored quickly, had good new-ball bowlers and guys who could keep it tight. And an outstanding captain who invariably made the right calls in the field. If Twenty20 had been around at the time we'd have won a lot more trophies.

Apart from leading Sussex to victory in the NatWest Final at Lord's in 1986, nothing gave me greater pleasure during my time at Hove than when we clinched the Sunday League title in front of 6,000 there against Middlesex and I scored 56 out of an opening stand of 134 with Gehan, who went on to make a century. There were people at Middlesex who had doubted my ability during my time there and also when I left. I had proved that in the right environment I could flourish. So much so that a few weeks later I was heading off to Australia for an Ashes series with the England squad and a year later playing in the World Cup.

As I said, but for the lack of a top-class spinner we would have won many more trophies over the next few years. But all the time we had Imran and Garth in our attack we had a chance in any game. It's funny when I see Imran the world statesman these days on TV, prime minister of Pakistan. You couldn't describe him as a political animal back in his Sussex days, although after he led them to victory in the 1992 World Cup I had a hunch he might end up in a position of authority in his country one day. As a fast bowler he had few equals. He was a natural athlete who was taught how to bowl an out-swinger by John Snow, when he came to Sussex from Worcestershire. He socialised as much as the rest of us, but he looked after himself. While the rest of us were falling over at the end of a long night he'd have long finished the couple of drinks he allowed himself before necking a pint of milk as a cure against a hangover.

In their pomp at Hove Imran and Garth were a frightening prospect. Many is the time I saw opposition batsmen turn up, take one look under the covers and declare themselves unfit. Peter Eaton, the groundsman, always left a good covering of grass on the wicket and would then get his assistant Bob Major to sit on the roller for hours and hours and hours, sometimes all day. I certainly improved as a wicketkeeper, even though I spent most of the time standing 30 yards back. Even when Imran and Garth took a breather, Tony Pigott, Adrian Jones and Ian Greig would all get the ball through at decent pace as well.

We had some fine batsmen too. Although Allan Green didn't fulfil his potential, Paul Parker and Alan Wells both played for England although I still think that they were picked after they had reached their peak. Alan and Colin, his elder brother, were cricket nuts and when I first saw Alan, I thought he was an outstanding prospect. He was brave against the short stuff and really strong off the back foot, which you needed to be to prosper on the Hove pitches. He had a couple of lean spells and at one stage Middlesex were keen to have him, but we stuck with him and he flourished. He was Sussex's most consistent batsman during that decade. Colin was a very decent all-rounder who played two one-day internationals for England in the mid-1980s and, in another era, might have played many more times for his country.

By 1986 John Barclay was struggling a bit with his finger, caused not by spinning the ball too hard but from fending off new-ball bowlers. I had stood in for John on a handful of occasions at the end of 1985 but I took over properly in May 1986 when we played Somerset in the Benson & Hedges Cup at Hove. Although we had a decent season in the John Player Sunday League, eventually finishing fourth, we struggled in the Championship and lost to Middlesex at Lord's in the quarter-final of the B&H. So by the end of June our last hope of any success was the NatWest Trophy.

In the first round we played Suffolk at Hove but when I walked out to toss I realised I didn't have a coin. I turned to Peter Eaton, who you didn't see with money too often, and when he dug into his pockets all he had was a two-pence piece. Anyway, we needed to win the toss because it wasn't one of his best wickets and we did. And from then on I kept the 2p with me and it turned out to be our lucky charm.

What made our success so surprising was that we won five games and only bowled 17 overs of spin in total. David Standing sent down 12 overs of off breaks against Suffolk and five when we defeated Glamorgan in the next round but apart from that I used our seamers.

We had a very individualistic side and my captaincy method was pretty simple really. I let the boys do their own thing, but I respected their input, certainly those guys who had played a bit. Imran and Garth were fantastic bowlers who knew what they wanted and I encouraged our batsmen to play their own way. In one-day cricket I really enjoyed the cut and thrust of captaincy. Where I found it more difficult was in the County Championship, keeping wicket and putting pressure on myself to do my bit with the bat as well. Those could be long days sometimes.

We beat Suffolk by seven wickets after I made what I still regard as one of my best-ever captaincy calls, not that it's a big list to choose from. We had a technically good batsman on the staff called Rehan Alikhan. In the Championship he would sometimes bat as low as seven or eight but in the NatWest, which was 60 overs in those days, I took a punt on him to open. The only instruction he had was to blunt the opposition's new-ball attack. I didn't need him to score quickly, we had plenty of players lower down who could do that. All he had to do was stay there.

Ray, as Rehan was always known in the dressing room, was one of the nicest men I've ever met in my life, but he was also the bravest or stupidest I've ever come across in cricket. He actually didn't mind getting hit. If he didn't walk off with a few more bruises he didn't think he had done his job. You have to remember in those days most counties had one or two very fine opening bowlers. Guys like Courtney Walsh were coming through and there were English quicks who could go through the gears like Norman Cowans and Syd Lawrence.

Allan Green scored the only hundred of the NatWest campaign when we beat Glamorgan by 29 runs at Hove in the second round but our luck in the draw didn't hold. The quarter-final was at Headingley, where the team we fielded was the one that took us all the way to the trophy: Alikhan, Green, Parker, Imran, Alan Wells, Colin Wells, Gould, Le Roux, Reeve, Pigott and Jones. Our preparation was hardly ideal. We finished a Championship game the night before at Guildford then drove up, and when I saw the wicket the next morning, which had been used a few weeks earlier for a Test match, I didn't think either team would make 100, it was that bad. It was horribly uneven and, to make matters worse, the clouds seemed to be hovering so low overhead it felt that you'd be able to reach up and touch them.

Although he wasn't playing, John Barclay had travelled with us. I was hell-bent on fielding first but he felt if we could get even 180 on the board with our seam attack in those conditions it would take some getting. Anyway, the lucky 2p worked again but after most of the first day had been lost to rain and bad light we struggled badly and were 86/6 when I played what I regard as my finest innings for Sussex.

I had a lot of luck early on and their captain David Bairstow took the seamers off when they were all over us. Phil Carrick came on to bowl his left-arm spin and that took the pressure off us a bit. Garth Le Roux and I put on 115 for the seventh wicket before I went for 88, which at the time was my highest score in one-day cricket. Yorkshire's target was 214 but they never got close. That was as well as I saw Sussex bowl in a one-day game during that era. We knocked them over for fun, bowling them out for 125 in 38.3 overs.

The weather at Headingley was nothing compared to the sight which greeted us when we turned up at New Road, Worcester for the semi-final, having made another dash up the motorway the previous night from Southampton. It looked like God's nightmare had arrived. The ground had been flooded and the pitch was wet. John Hick, Graeme's dad, erected canopies over the square and blasted hot air underneath because he'd used the same methods to dry out tobacco on his farm in Zimbabwe. When that didn't work a bloke in a helicopter started hovering over the square to help dry it out as well, although that was a complete waste of fuel.

We were very lucky because Roy Palmer and Don Oslear were the umpires and they were sticklers for the regulations. In those days some umpires wouldn't worry too much if water had got under the covers and the run-ups were a bit damp. They had three spinners in their side and we didn't have one so I was forever in the umpires' earholes about the conditions and, to their credit, they made sure it was fit before we eventually started. I won the toss again and put them in but we didn't make a great start. On what was the second day they were 66/1 when I brought on Colin Wells and Dermot Reeve who took pace off the ball, bowled cutters and were virtually unplayable. They eventually cobbled together 125 and on day three we finished off winning by five wickets, Ray Alikhan having made 41 from something like 150 balls.

A week before the semi-final I had injured my hand in a Championship game at Eastbourne. Dermot took over the gloves and I took my only wickets in first-class cricket against Derbyshire but then three weeks before the final I aggravated an old hip injury during the warm-up before a Sunday League match against Kent. Stupidly, I played, and got 65, but by the end I was in agony. Even a week before Lord's I was touch and go but I had some very intensive massage treatment and played a club game for Brighton Brunswick, scored a few runs and next day felt fine.

For a lot of our guys a Lord's final was a new experience and when we travelled up the day before I could sense a few nerves. So instead of nets I ordered the coach driver to take us to a quiet pub I knew near Slough called The Pheasant, and we had a couple of drinks together to relax. Unconventional I know, but it did the trick because in the final we played out of our skin.

Conditions for September finals at Lord's invariably make the toss crucial but I realised we had an advantage even when I walked out. Lancashire had opted to play Clive Lloyd instead of Patrick Patterson, their very fearsome opening bowler, even though Clive was 42 and this was to be his final major game. Clive is one of the nicest people I've met in cricket and he had been a great servant to Lancashire, but his time was up. When we found out he was playing instead of Patterson it definitely lifted the spirits.

The 2p coin worked again and I stuck them in but we struggled with the ball. Gehan Mendis, who'd left us to join Lancashire in 1985, and Graeme Fowler gave them a good start and even guys like Garth seemed to be overawed by the occasion. But then when he walked back to field on the boundary someone in the crowd threw a blonde wig at Garth, who was losing his hair and was a bit touchy about it. The lads all saw this, pissed themselves laughing and it seemed to relax us. We gave Clive a guard of honour, not only as a gesture as it was his final innings at Lord's but also because I thought it might distract him. It worked. Dermot Reeve got him first ball and, although their 242/8 was the fifth-0highest score in Lord's finals, we fancied our chances on what was a good batting wicket.

Allan Green and Paul Parker built a platform for us and both went on to make half-centuries before Imran and Colin Wells finished it off, Colin hitting Mike Watkinson for six to seal victory with a couple of overs to spare. Needless to say we celebrated long and hard. It was a magical day. On a personal level, going back to the place where I'd played a lot of cricket and leading my team out in a major final and winning, it was a dream come true, it really was.

I had hopes for 1987 but things began to unravel very quickly. I kept telling myself that a series of mishaps and mistakes was nothing to do with my appointment as captain, but halfway through the summer I wasn't so sure. It all started in the winter when the committee decided to sack the coach Stewart Storey. Stewart was a decent coach and a very good administrator but the committee took soundings from a few of the players and decided he had to go. I was gutted for the bloke, but when the committee discussed his future I kept quiet – something I still regret today. I apologised the next time I saw Stewart, and he accepted it with good grace, but the damage had been done.

John Jameson was put in charge of coaching but it was a very loose arrangement, and during the season

Ian Thomson, John Snow and Jim Parks helped out. All three had been Sussex greats of course, but the younger players couldn't relate to these guys at all. Dermot Reeve had joined Warwickshire, Imran was with Pakistan and it was Garth's last season and he was a shadow of the bowler he had been a few years earlier.

I was struggling with a knee injury, which didn't help, and then Paul Parker had his arm broken by Wayne Daniel early in the season and missed a couple of months. One of the young batsmen coming through was Neil Lenham, but Daniel fractured Neil's finger in the same match and later in the season his foot was broken against Yorkshire at Sheffield. The atmosphere around the place was terrible. I finally flipped at a committee meeting when the subject of squad rebuilding was deferred after a long discussion so we could talk about two seemingly more important matters: a complaint that the toilet paper in the ladies wasn't soft enough and the lack of fairy cakes on the menu in the pavilion at tea. I threw my pen on the table and stormed out. And when the minutes of the meeting were sent, my little tantrum had been duly recorded.

I should probably have given up halfway through the season. It was affecting my form with the gloves and bat and I was miserable at home. By the time it got to August I didn't even want to play at all. Jo insisted I go and see Alan Wadey and he was brilliant. I was due a benefit in 1990 so I didn't want to do anything daft. I didn't want to leave because I was still an important member of the team so it was a relief a few weeks later when the club offered me a new three-year contract and a benefit, which eventually raised £110,000 and enabled me to pay off my mortgage and give me a bit of financial security for the first time in my life.

Paul Parker took over as captain and when Norman Gifford joined him as coach in 1989 things started to pick up. They got the old spirit back and the changing room was much happier, but with uncapped players generally outnumbering capped players each time we took to the field results only improved slowly. Imran had gone, after more than 7,000 runs and 400 wickets for Sussex, but some decent younger players like Peter Moores and Martin Speight emerged along with Neil Lenham. Before he left, Imran recommended Waqar Younis to us but instead the committee signed Tony Dodemaide, a wholehearted Australian fast bowler who gave Sussex some good years. But he was no Waqar Younis.

It was a tough gig for Paul, but I don't think he ever got the credit for how well he steadied the ship and began the rebuilding process, although in my opinion it was another ten years, following the revolution led by Tony Pigott, before Sussex really sorted themselves out. Paul was a fantastic batsman. In another era he would have played 50 Test matches. He dovetailed well with Norman Gifford. 'Giff' didn't say a lot – you knew when he was unhappy because he started puffing on his pipe more quickly – but when he did speak it usually made sense. He knew the game inside out.

By 1991, after 17 seasons in the first-class game, I'd had enough of playing. I had completed my coaching badges and began making plans for the end of the season, when I would retire. I quite fancied becoming a cricket coach at a private school and had no intention of leaving Sussex. We had a young family and Jo and I, who married in 1987, were very settled in the area.

Then, out of the blue, Don Bennett rang and invited me to run the second team at Middlesex. I spoke to Sussex but they weren't keen to release me from my contract, which I'd extended for another year. I was pleased someone had effectively made the decision for me but as the season got underway Middlesex's offer looked more attractive. At the end of April we went up to Edgbaston to play Warwickshire in the Sunday League. I was in the team, but before we'd tossed it rained and, as the overs were reduced, I wasn't going to play and then I was. In the end we had a 10-over slog and I came in at no.3 and made 21 before being run out. During the rain delay I'd been chatting to Keith Piper, the Warwickshire wicketkeeper, about Middlesex's approach and just before I was dismissed Allan Donald bowled a ball so quickly, I literally didn't see it. By the time I played a shot the ball was in Keith's gloves. At the end of the over he jogged past me and said: 'Gunner, if I was you, I'd take that job.'

So a few days later I spoke to Paul Parker and Giff and explained that I wanted to go, not least because I could see I was holding up Peter Moores's development.

The club eventually agreed and less than a month later I was making my second Middlesex debut, as player-coach, against Hampshire seconds at Harrow. I would stay at a hotel owned by a mate of mine in Marble Arch during the week and commute back to Hove at the weekend.

Had I not returned to Middlesex, I would probably never have had the fantastic career in umpiring I subsequently enjoyed, but it was only a few weeks in when I realised I'd made a big mistake. Whoever said 'never go back' was absolutely spot on.

9

England

I HAVE never been one to blow my own trumpet, and when I began my career as an international umpire in 2006 and I would chat to the fielder at square leg or the non-striker while on the field there would invariably be a surprised reaction if I happened to mention that yes, I have played for my country.

I am much more well known around the world for what I've done wearing a white coat rather than my achievements wearing white flannels, but no one is going to take away from me that in 1982 and 1983 I played 22 times for England – four first-class matches during an Ashes tour and 18 one-day internationals – including the 1983 World Cup when England reached the semi-final.

I have to be honest. I probably owed my selection for the World Cup and the tour to Australia and New Zealand in the winter of 1982/83 which preceded it to two things. Alan Knott was serving a three-year ban after going on a rebel tour to South Africa early in 1982 (before you wonder, I wasn't asked) and my good form in one-day cricket for Sussex during 1982, when I opened the batting with Gehan Mendis and we won the Sunday League by a record margin. Bob Taylor was the senior wicketkeeper, and the only way I was going to play in any of the Tests, as England tried to defend the Ashes so famously won in 1981, was if Bob got injured. And there wasn't much chance of that happening. Bob may have been 41 when the tour got underway, but he kept himself supremely fit. His work ethic quite frankly embarrassed a few of the younger lads including myself and, along with Knotty, he was still one of the best wicketkeepers in the world.

Looking back now – and bearing in mind the 13 years I subsequently experienced at the heart of international cricket as an umpire – I can only describe the England set-up when I played as amateurish. There were some fine players around though, several of whom, in my opinion, would have made the England team which won the World Cup for the first time in 2019. But you simply cannot compare what happened then with what goes on now. Cricket at that time was still organised more like it was the 1920s than the 2020s.

What an honour though, and one I had absolutely no idea was coming my way. Back then touring parties were announced before the end of the season and I subsequently found out from Bob Willis, who had succeeded Mike Brearley as captain, that he liked that I wasn't a moaner. I was sociable, I knew what my role would be and I wouldn't rock the boat. In short, I would be a good tourist. My job wasn't even to put Bob Taylor under pressure for his place. I just had to keep ticking over and when the Benson & Hedges World Series Cup started after the Tests – ten games involving Australia, New Zealand and England – I would get my chance. There was also a three-match series in New Zealand straight after the World Series Cup finished and we even stopped off in Sharjah at Ian Botham's insistence on the way back to play a one-off game against Pakistan. The hospitality there was very good but if there was a few extra quid for playing what was effectively an exhibition match I didn't see any of it.

Those 13 one-day internationals should have given us good preparation for the World Cup, which was only three months away when we got back, but the tournament was hardly ever mentioned when we were in Australia or New Zealand. We lived from day to day, match to match. Forward planning generally revolved around what we would get up to in the evenings.

The way I discovered my selection sums up how things were done in those days. I was in the 147 Snooker Club in Hove when a call came through for me on the payphone by the tables. To this day I didn't know who it was at the other end of the line. Peter May had taken over as chairman of selectors, but it wasn't him. I'd heard an interview he did when he had taken over from Alec Bedser and I would have recognised his voice. Anyway, I didn't believe whoever it was when they told me I'd been picked. I thought it was a wind-up by one of the Sussex lads. It was only when I realised that Ian Greig, the person most likely to have made the prank call, was playing snooker with Garth Le Roux in front of me that I thought it might not have been a hoax.

A few minutes later John Vinicombe, the sportswriter on the Brighton *Evening Argus*, got hold of me at the snooker club and offered his congratulations. Even then I didn't believe him. John had to come down with the story ripped off the news wires and wave the bit of paper with the list of players in the party in front of me. After giving John chapter and verse for his story I got very drunk to celebrate. It was probably the biggest shock I've had during 40-plus years in the game. I had read a few articles in the papers leading up to the squad's announcement, but I still didn't think I had a chance of going. I was more concerned with trying to avoid another winter earning a few quid on the building site when the season ended. Jo was probably more thrilled about the news than me and my dad loved it. When he went to his social club in Cippenham that night for a pint his mates bought him drinks all evening to celebrate.

There was no pre-tour fitness camp or anything like that. Instead, we all met up at physiotherapist Bernard Thomas's practice in Birmingham where he checked our blood pressure before we were fitted out for our tour blazers. And that was that. It was only then, when I was in the same room as guys like Ian Botham, David Gower and Allan Lamb, that I realised what an honour it was. Obviously, I'd played against these lads many times but now they were going to be team-mates. One thing I did realise as I looked around the room was that it would be a very sociable tour.

And a long one. We played our first game on 22 October against Queensland in Brisbane, three weeks before the first Test, although I was lucky not to be sent home by then. The one thing I remember about the very long flight to Perth was that Robin Jackman had got enough duty-free cigarettes to get him through the interminable journey and I hadn't. That's right, smoking was allowed on a plane back then. I don't think David Boon's record for the amount of cans of beer consumed on a pre-Ashes tour flight was ever threatened, but we had a few drinks and then when we got to the hotel, Bernard Thomas told us to stay up as long as we could to try to counter the effects of jet lag. A few us needed no second invitation and enjoyed ourselves through until early morning in the hotel bar before going to bed.

I must have stumbled over the note Bernard had pushed under my bedroom door to tell us that there would be a running session on a nearby school field the next day because I turned up late and certainly wasn't in the leading group of runners as we did laps of the field under the hot sun. As we walked off Bernard collared me. 'Do that again, and you'll be on the first plane home.' It might seem strange that I was being lectured by the physio and not the coach but that's because there wasn't a coach as such. Peter May was there as chairman of selectors, although he didn't turn up until the Test series started and certainly didn't stay for the one-day stuff, Doug Insole was tour manager and Norman Gifford's title was assistant coach. Then there was Bernard the physio and our scorer – and that was it.

Bernard sorted the accommodation out and my room-mate was Bob Taylor but I don't think we lasted more than a week together. He was a nice, tidy, charming guy who kept good hours and had been lumbered with a loudmouth who came back to the room at all hours. So the management decided I should share with Robin Jackman instead and my initial thoughts when I heard this were not happy ones. Quite frankly, I'd have rather slept on the lobby floor.

I had played against Robin for Surrey and hitherto had regarded him as another of those posh, public-school-educated idiots with a sense of entitlement. I'd been on a benefit tour the year before and got to know him a little better, but I still wasn't sure about Robin, especially as a room-mate for the next four months or so. But within a couple of days together I realised I'd got him totally wrong. Not only was he one of the funniest men I have ever met in cricket, he would do anything for you. He sewed buttons on my shirt, made me endless cups of tea, kept me company in the bar when everyone else had gone to bed and went for walks with me when the last thing he wanted to do was leave the room. Neither of us played much cricket on that tour so we kept each other going and made sure we didn't get too down on ourselves. Jackers was not much more than a glorified net bowler on that trip while I spent a lot of the time ferrying drinks and spare gloves on to the field, but he never complained. I used to see him regularly when I umpired in Cape Town and, nearly 40 years later, we still keep in touch.

I didn't play in any of the three warm-up games before the first Test in Perth, which was drawn and became famous because a bloke climbed over the fence, cuffed Terry Alderman on the head and was then rugby-tackled to the ground by Terry, who dislocated his shoulder in the process. We flew to Sydney and it was at the Sydney Cricket Ground on 20 November, in a four-day match against New South Wales, that I made my first appearance for England. I did okay, scoring 73 in the first innings in a match we won by

26 runs. But I was hit on the thumb in the nets and Bob Taylor had to keep wicket in their second innings.

The difference between the two teams in the Tests was the quality of the bowling attacks. Even without Alderman and the injured Dennis Lillee, Jeff Thomson, Geoff Lawson and Rodney Hogg took 67 wickets between them. Bob Willis and Ian Botham took 18 apiece but our next best bowler was off-spinner Geoff Miller with 13. 'Both' had yet to convince the Australians that he was the world's best all-rounder, despite his heroics in the 1981 series in England, and he had a poor tour with the bat by his very high standards. In 38 innings his top score was 65 and I'm not sure how fit he was. He had a few injury niggles, had put a bit of weight on and, with his young family in tow, was allowed to stay away from the main tour party quite a bit of the time. But he was still golden bollocks and had a knack of getting us a wicket when we needed one although he didn't win us a match through his own endeavours, which we'd probably expected him to do.

He did have time for the young players though and when he organised a night out he made sure everyone was there. We took our cricket very seriously, but when the opportunity arose to let our hair down we grabbed it. The only sensible one among us was Chris Tavare, who did okay in the Test series despite being forced to open when his best position was no.3.

The only time I thought I might have a chance of playing in a Test came when Derek Randall was hit on the head by Michael Holding, who was playing for Tasmania, during a one-day match in Launceston between the third and fourth Tests. It wasn't a deliberate ploy by Mikey, the ball just reared up horribly off a length on a terribly uneven wicket. He refused to bowl short after that, much to the displeasure of his captain, and just sent down medium-paced yorkers. Derek staggered off and initially it didn't look good, but after a couple of days he recovered, and we headed to Melbourne for what is still considered one of the best-ever Ashes Test matches.

I played my part too. Graeme Fowler was struck on the toe by Jeff Thomson and couldn't field and the 12th man options weren't great. Vic Marks wasn't much of an athlete, Jackers could only do fine leg at both ends and Geoff Cook was struggling with a rib injury. That left me, and I loved it.

The first-day crowd was about 65,000 and I ended up fielding down at third man in front of Bay 13, Melbourne's equivalent of the notorious hill at

Sydney. I think most of the punters turned up pissed because by mid-afternoon it was starting to get a bit lively with more than the occasional beer can tossed in my direction, not all of them empty. There was a drinks break and I decided not to bother because it meant running 90-odd yards in the heat and I wasn't thirsty anyway. So I exchanged a few pleasantries with the crowd and then, with my back to them, leaned on the advertising hoardings. The next thing I know I felt this horrible splattering on the back of my head. One of the punters had landed a dinner plate-sized Four'n Twenty pie on to my hair, complete with a helping of tomato sauce.

The other boys heard the commotion and turned around to see everyone in Bay 13 pointing at me. To make matters worse, I cleaned my hands in the gutter behind the boards without realising it was the piss from the toilets. There was no time to go back to the changing room and for the rest of the session I tried to get rid of the worst of the pie by running my hands through my hair between deliveries. By tea my hair had crusted up under the hot Melbourne sun, and with red streaks I looked, as Robin Jackman sagely observed, like the first punk rocker to play for England. I washed it all out but Bob Willis still sent me down to field in front of Bay 13 for the rest of the day, to the delight of the crowd and my team-mates.

The other moment in that Test I will always remember was my catch to dismiss Greg Chappell for just two runs when Australia began their chase of 292 for victory. Norman Cowans bowled a back-of-a-length delivery and all I could hear was this agitated cry of 'Shit' from Greg as the ball lobbed up towards me in the covers. I thought it was going to be a simple catch but as the ball died on me I ended up having to dive forward and grab it before being mobbed by the rest of the team. These days it would be regarded as a straightforward catch. Back then *Wisden* described it as 'spectacular'.

When last man Jeff Thomson walked out to join Allan Border, Australia were 218/9. Border had been using a bat made by an Australian company called Symonds but had hardly scored a run with it. Ian Botham got him out for two in the first innings and, whether it was an act of kindness towards his mate or even pity I don't know, but he gave Allan one of his Duncan Fearnley bats. Now, suddenly, Border started smacking the ball all over the Melbourne Cricket Ground. Bob Willis quickly decided that the only batsman we were going to get out was Thommo, so he spread the field and allowed Allan easy runs. In the first innings Thommo was bowled having a wild swing at Geoff Miller, but he grew in confidence and by the close of the fourth day the target was down to 37.

We were still strong favourites, but 18,000 spectators turned up hoping to see a miracle the next morning. We had the new ball up our sleeve, but if I'm honest I never thought we were going to get Thomson out, while Border continued to play with supreme confidence. Then in the 18th over of the day, Ian got one to nip away, Chris Tavare parried what was a straightforward catch at second slip and Geoff Miller had the presence of mind to take a couple of steps behind him from first slip and grab the ball about 18 inches off the ground. We had won by three runs. When we came off no one said anything for about 15 minutes. Then we let our hair down. It was a wonderful experience to be part of until we realised that we'd all brought our flights forward 24 hours and there was a mad scramble to get our plane to Sydney.

The final Test ended in a draw but we might have won had it not been for the worst example of not concentrating by an umpire I ever saw on a cricket pitch when Australia opener John Dyson was reprieved by the umpire Mel Johnson after he'd been run out in the first over by a foot-and-a-half. We couldn't believe it at the time and, even when Johnson was shown TV replays of his error, he said he'd given Dyson, who went on to score a crucial 79, the benefit of the doubt. If you don't believe me, have a look on YouTube.

Anyway, the serious stuff was now starting for me, or so I thought. For the four days between the end of the Test and the opening one-day match against Australia I practised as hard as I'd done at any time in my career, so it came as a bit of a shock at the team meeting when Doug Insole named Bob Taylor in the team for the first one-dayer instead of me. But I got my head down again and after we lost the first two games I finally made my full England debut in Brisbane on 15 January 1983 opening with Chris Tavare. There was no ceremony. As far as the management were concerned, I'd been given my England kit when we'd all met up at Bernard Thomas's before the tour and I simply got on with it.

New Zealand opened the bowling with Richard Hadlee and a guy called Gary Troup, who I'd played against during my spell with Auckland a couple of years earlier. Hadlee demanded respect of course because he was world-class, but it was Troup who I couldn't lay a bat on. I made 15 out of an opening stand of 26 and then gave a slip catch to Geoff Howarth and left the stage for David Gower to make an imperious 158 as we won by 54 runs. The following day I was run out for two in the first over as we lost to Australia.

I opened in one more game, batted once at six and when I made 42 – my highest score for England – against the Australians in Sydney I came in at seven with Trevor Jesty, who had flown in as cover for the injured Randall, at six. After we failed to reach the final, we flew to New Zealand for three more one-day internationals, all of which we lost, where I twice batted at seven and then opened in the final game. It was a complete mess. No one was thinking any further forward than the next match and by the time we reached New Zealand for that mini-series all everyone wanted to do was fly home. We arrived back in England on 2 March, having been away for more than five months.

My own scores with the bat had been pretty modest but I felt I had kept wicket well. However, when I returned to Sussex, I made low scores in two Sunday League games opening and in the Benson & Hedges Cup, which was 50 overs, I batted in the middle order. So it came as a pleasant surprise when

I was named in the squad for the World Cup, which took place over a fortnight in mid-June in brilliant weather. The tournament back then was nothing like the extravaganza it became but our approach was even then pretty amateurish. We travelled between games in cars, while the other teams were transported around in plush coaches, and when we turned up for the official photograph at Lord's before the tournament started all of the teams were dressed in matching suits, except us. We looked like a collection of tailor's dummies straight out of a shop window.

I remember one morning in the hotel before a game in Taunton when Peter May, who'd never had a proper conversation with me before, came over at breakfast. I think he knew my name, although he never called me Ian. Instead, he asked what college I'd gone to and what my role was in the side! If I'd have told him I'd gone to Oxford, opened the bowling and batted in the top three I don't think dear old PBH would have been any the wiser.

Despite the somewhat chaotic nature of our preparations we had a good side and, until the semifinal at least, the benefit of playing regularly in English conditions. Bob Willis was still in charge and, as had been the case in Australia, he was happy to let the senior players have a big say in tactics. We won our first game against New Zealand by 106 runs and, although they beat us in the second meeting, we won five out of six in the group stages to reach the semi-finals. I kept well and scored 35 against Sri Lanka, although in most of the matches I wasn't needed to bat. We had a strong top order and in a 60-over game our best players had time to build their innings.

On the way from the Sri Lanka game in Taunton to London to play Pakistan we decided to have a pit stop in Bray near the Thames where some friends of Allan Lamb and I lived. By the time we got to Lord's for 4pm practice most of us were pretty pissed. The fielding session was embarrassingly bad. Poor old Bob Willis couldn't believe it, but the next day we hammered Pakistan by eight wickets and produced what was easily our best performance of the tournament.

Our worst was in the semi-final against India at Old Trafford. It was only mid-June but the groundsman Bert Flack, who would roll animal intestines from the nearby abattoir into the square as part of his preparations, produced a dry, flaky pitch which was more like something you might find in Madras than Manchester. It was tailor-made for their medium pacers like Roger Binny, Madan Lal and Mohinder Amarnath, although we were 84/1 in the 21st over before we subsided to 213 all out. My own contribution – which you can watch on YouTube – was to be 'ingloriously run out', as Tom Graveney describes it in the BBC commentary, for 13. India eased to victory by six wickets and that was that. The squad split the £4,000 prize money for reaching the semi-finals and that night Trevor Jesty dropped me off in Basingstoke on his way home to Southampton and I joined up with the rest of the Sussex team and did 12th man duties for the remainder of our County Championship match against Hampshire.

I never played for England again to no one's great surprise, least of all mine. I wasn't consistent with the bat. Although I had a settled place in the batting order at seven during the World Cup I knew, deep down, that I wasn't good enough and you can't approach international sport, whatever it is, and hope to succeed with that mindset.

I guess it's only in recent years that I have come to appreciate the England career I did have, modest though my achievements were. I played with some fantastic players. Guys like David Gower, Ian Botham and the late Bob Willis, whose death at the end of 2019 came as a great shock to me, would have played in any England team in any era. I never got anywhere near their standards, but I had a wonderful time.

Jane Admans and I, winners of the Slough Observer *Young Sportsperson of the Year awards. Did we really wear shirts with lapels that size back then?*

I was a bit older when I won another award from the Slough Observer

Early days in the Arsenal youth team

On tour with the young Gunners in Tehran, Iran, before the revolution I hasten to add! I think the guy standing on the left was our security guard

Arsenal reserves at Highbury in 1974. David O'Leary and Graham Rix, who both had great careers with the club, are in the back row with me

Making a save for Arsenal during the final of the tournament in Iran. I wasn't the tallest, but my handling and bravery were never questioned

Standing next to Mike Gatting for this Middlesex pre-season photo in the mid-1970s. Note, the snow on the ground!

Hitting out against Yorkshire at Lord's, the late David Bairstow looks on admiringly

Running out Warwickshire's Rohan Kanhai in a match at Lord's with Graham Barlow at point about to start the celebrations

Early days at Sussex with John Barclay, who was a great captain and wonderful person, and Ian Greig

On the attack in my early days at Hove

MCC secretary Jack Bailey, with whom I had a few run-ins in my early days at Middlesex, looks on as I receive the NatWest Trophy at Lord's in 1986

Nearly running out Neil Fairbrother in the 1986 NatWest Final against Lancashire

Celebrations at Lord's with Sussex after we won the 1986 NatWest Trophy. Garth Le Roux's father (in glasses) hijacked the party!

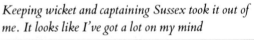

My wicketkeeping improved a lot when I joined Sussex, but Imran Khan and Garth Le Roux hit the gloves hard

Keeping wicket and captaining Sussex took it out of me. It looks like I've got a lot on my mind

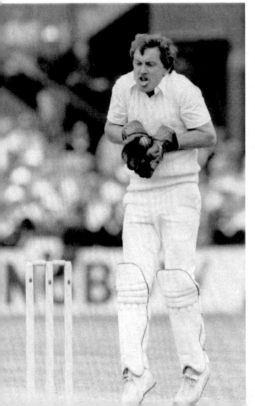

This year's beneficiary, Ian Gould, writes:

ussex — best move
could have made...

● IAN GOULD — enjoys life

Racing helped me escape from cricket pressures and I met a friend for life in Josh Gifford, who wrote some nice words in my benefit magazine

Gifford's tip: Put money on Gunner

JOSH GIFFORD is president of Ian Gould's benefit. This is the Sussex trainer on the subject of Gunner:

Now and then he enjoys a day at the races and having the odd flutter! He also takes a keen interest in our horses and has occasionally been to Findon to watch them at exercise, where he doesn't miss much either. But that is not the reason I accepted when he asked me to be president of his benefit year.

It always amazes me just how many of the cricketers, past and present, who love racing.

I have many friends in cricket whom I have met because of their great interest in my sport. I always try to give them good tips, but trainers are notoriously bad tipsters, and I am no exception.

I suppose a day at the races for them is a relaxation, as a day on the cricket field, or watching at Lord's or Hove, is a great day for

me. I can think of nothing better.

When my son, as a young lad, was lucky enough to go to the county ground at Hove for coaching, there he found Ian very friendly and helpful. His genuine interest in all the other boys, the encouragement he gave them to develop their skills, and the obvious dedication and the time he gives to the job, brought it home to me what a great example he is to other cricketers and what an asset to Sussex.

This must augur well for the club's future. Ian's also shows a willingness to play wherever and whenever possible in various charity games, and you can always count on him, as I have done on many occasions.

This year Sussex have rewarded Ian Gould's loyalty and dedication by granting him a benefit. I hope every supporter will acknowledge his service by responding generously.

From all of us here at Findon, we wish him a very successful and enjoyable year.

● JOSH GIFFORD

Flat out at Hove. In the end, the chance to return to Middlesex as a coach proved irresistible. I'd had enough of playing

About to head to the West Indies with the England Young Cricketers. I got back in time to help Middlesex celebrate winning the County Championship in 1975

Resplendent in our powder blue kit, the England squad for the World Series Cup in Australia in 1983 when I made my international debut

Running out Javed Miandad, who was acting as runner for my Sussex team-mate Imran Khan, in the 1983 World Cup match against Pakistan at Lord's. Our preparations had involved a lot of beer drinking the day before but it was our best performance of the tournament

Walking out at The Oval with Darrell Hair to umpire my first international match against Sri Lanka in 2006. A very proud day

Watching the rain fall at the Sydney Cricket Ground in 2016 during the Australia versus West Indies series. You're right, the umpires' rooms there aren't the biggest!

Chatting with the Afghanistan players in Nagpur during the 2016 T20 World Cup

David Warner and I during the Australia versus India Test a few days after Phil Hughes had died. We had our moments, but Davey is a decent man and a fine player

Cape Town 2018. Richard Illingworth and Nigel Llong in discussion with Cameron Bancroft and Steve Smith

Seeing the funny side with India's Virat Kohli and Rishabh Pant and umpire Marais Erasmus during the 2018 series against Australia in Melbourne. In hindsight, I wish that had been my last Test match

A hug from Virat Kohli after my final international – the World Cup game between India and Sri Lanka at Headingley in 2019

A nice moment on my final day as colleagues joined me to commiserate and celebrate in equal 29! From left, Paul Reiffel, Chris Broad, Chris Gaffaney, Rod Tucker, Nigel Llong, Paul Wilson, Bruce Oxenford and David Boon

Walking out at Potchefstroom with Roly Black and Sam Nogajski before the Under-19 World Cup match between Zimbabwe and Scotland early in 2020. The opportunity to stand in five games and mentor some of the new recruits was something I really enjoyed

My three grandchildren, Mya, left, Neo, top right, and Ava.

With Jo, my rock for the last 40 years

At Hove early in 2020, about to start my 20th season on the county circuit

The Gould first team on my last day as an international umpire at Headingley in 2019. From left: Michael, me, Jo, Gemma and George

10

Never Go Back

URING the last couple of years of my playing career I made up my mind that, if possible, I wanted to stay in the game, but I just wasn't sure in what role.

Umpiring never really crossed my mind if I'm being honest. While I was still playing, one or two of the younger members of the Sussex squad would seek my advice on little technical things about their game and I found that I quite enjoyed passing on my experience and knowledge. So coaching was the next logical step and I started attending winter nets at Hove and helping out guys like Les Lenham – who was a superb coach and whose advice was still being sought by some of the Sussex players 25 years later – with some of the younger players in the squad.

Pat Cale and Chris Waller, who I had played with, were also good coaches in their own right and I did a few one-to-one sessions with Les's son Neil who, had it not been for injuries and in particular broken bones, would have played for England in my opinion. I went up to the old National Sports Centre at Lilleshall in Shropshire where Les and Graham Saville ran coaching courses for the Test and County Cricket Board – the forerunner of the ECB – and I did my various qualifications. There were quite a few other senior players there getting towards the end of their career who were thinking similarly to me and they were great weeks. I enjoyed learning and, of course, I enjoyed socialising in the evening. The trouble with cricket is that there are only so many coaching jobs, and certainly far fewer then than these days when most counties have a backroom staff as big as some of the Premier League football clubs.

The other thing I was interested in was groundsmanship. My imagination had been fired in New Zealand when part of my duties, at both the Ellerslie and Cornwall cricket clubs where I played in the 1980s, was looking after the outfield and preparing the square. I have always loved the outdoors and I enjoyed tinkering with machinery too. When people turned up at the weekend to play and congratulated me on the wicket I had prepared or the condition of the outfield I got a lot of satisfaction.

Michael and George both attended Windsor Boys' School and the school knew I had done some ground maintenance work and they asked me to look after the pitches. They played all the traditional school sports there, but the facilities when I started had been neglected for a while. So I borrowed machinery, sometimes from Eton College up the road, and began to look after the football and cricket pitches on a part-time basis for free.

Working at the school and eventually setting up my own grounds maintenance business was a big turning point in my life. It enabled me to escape from the cricket bubble I'd been part of for so long and meet people from totally different walks of life, all of whom seemed to lead far more interesting lives than I did. The headmaster was a lovely guy called Jeff Dawkins and he had some great teachers, who would work long hours after classes had finished to lay on sports coaching and games for the boys for no extra pay. The school ended up producing a lot of kids who played for the local clubs and some went on to achieve even greater prominence in sports like rowing and rugby.

The pitches were built on old allotments so there was a lot of work to be done. Even when I became second-team coach at Middlesex I still had quite a bit of time on my hands so eventually, as well as working at the school during the winter, I'd help out in the summer, getting there at 6am just when the sun was coming up and spending two or three hours sitting happily on a tractor, pushing the mower or rolling the wicket. After doing it for nothing for a while the school offered me a full-time job. I couldn't commit to that because of my Middlesex duties but I told them I would find someone to help me.

The school had a new pavilion built around this time and to this day I still go there during the summer and paint it for them, something I will carry on doing all the time I can pick up a paintbrush. Although I never considered a teaching career myself, I did take the occasional PE lesson if one of the teachers was sick. Sometimes Mr Dawkins would send a few errant pupils over to me and we'd have a chat. They would help me out for an hour with the pitches and, when they realised I wasn't a teacher and was someone they could talk to about problems at home or with academic stuff, we would try to work something out. Gunner the counsellor – who'd have thought it? On the odd occasion I even let them go outside the school to have a cigarette or two. Come to think of it, that's probably why I was quite popular.

Even now, when I go back to Berkshire, I still occasionally bump into some of those boys and we have a catch-up about those times. A few even thank me now for helping put them back on the straight and narrow. Hearing that makes me very proud.

In 1994 I started Gould Turfcare, which is still going strong more than 25 years later. Lewis Clements was the boyfriend of my niece Kerry. He was a printer who had been made redundant, so I offered him a few hours working with me at the school. I used to play football with his father Brian, and Lewis seemed like a nice guy. He turned up the following Monday and he's still there now, running the business with my youngest son George. I'm proud to say they have won a lot of awards for their groundsmanship and the company has a really good reputation in the Thames Valley area. I'm still a director to this day and help out when I am needed while Jo is company secretary.

If Don Bennett hadn't offered me the job coaching Middlesex's second team, I suspect I would have had a couple more years at most playing for Sussex before going into groundsmanship full time.

But if I'd taken that path, I don't think I would have had the third and most fulfilling part of my cricket career, umpiring. So in that respect I owe Middlesex a lot but for most of that decade, from 1990 onwards, I didn't think that way if I'm honest. Going back to Lord's was a very frustrating experience and rarely fulfilling, especially in the last few years I was there. Looking back now, I don't know how I did it for as long as I did.

When I returned to the club, Middlesex were a very strong side. They had finished third in the County Championship in 1989 and reached the final of the NatWest Trophy but that was considered a disappointing season by their standards. Mike Gatting, the captain, could call upon Desmond Haynes, Mark Ramprakash, Mike Roseberry, Roland Butcher, Paul Downton, John Emburey, Norman Cowans, Angus Fraser, Phil Tufnell and Simon Hughes among others and in 1990 they won the Championship and did so again in 1993. Inevitably, there were England call-ups during this successful period and when that happened it was my job to make sure the players coming in from the second team, even if it might only be for a couple of games while a Test match was on, were ready to make the step up.

Lord's itself had changed for the better in the decade or so since I had left and the atmosphere was a lot less stuffy but Middlesex were still very much poor relations. It was bad enough playing our games all over the place, but there wasn't anywhere permanent for the second team to practise either, and with most of the players living a fair distance from Lord's because central London was too expensive for them to live we had to beg, steal and borrow places to train. Even the indoor facilities at Lord's were off-limits if there was an international match on because they were given over to corporate hospitality guests.

I used some local contacts and trained at Slough CC for a while which was fine until we were instructed that we had to train in Middlesex itself. We tried a couple of the big Middlesex League clubs but got nowhere and it was proving extremely difficult until I met a guy called Dave New, who looked after the pitches at the RAF facility in Vine Lane, Uxbridge. The square there was hardly ever used so we started training and eventually playing games there. In fact, the facilities were much better than those up the road at Uxbridge CC where Middlesex's first team still play to this day.

I had taken over from Clive Radley, who had done a good job with the seconds by winning trophies and producing players and Don Bennett respected my opinion of a player which made life easier. There were some very good young players emerging in the early 1990s who were probably too good for second-team cricket but not quite ready for regular first-team exposure, or those who couldn't get a regular run in the team because when the England boys returned they rightly got their spot back. One player who fell into this category was a left-arm spinner called Alex Barnett who took wickets galore in the early 1990s for the seconds but who was never going to dislodge Phil Tufnell. Alex eventually left and joined Lancashire in search of more opportunities. Similarly, Jamie Sykes was a fine off-spinner but was never going to take the place of John Emburey.

During my time I worked with some very fine players: Andrew Strauss, Ben Hutton, Jamie Dalrymple, Owais Shah, Ed Joyce, Paul Weekes, Richard Johnson, Matthew Keech, David Nash, David Goodchild, Keith Dutch and Jason Pooley to name but a few. Some, of course, went on to have good careers with the county but others didn't fulfil their potential, although not many were keen on moving to another county even if their route into the first team seemed blocked off. Middlesex were a big club who paid well and although the second team never played at Lord's – and hardly ever practised there either – being part of the set-up which was based at the most famous cricket ground in the world carried some weight.

You could tell straightaway Andrew Strauss had serious talent. He came to us in 1996, halfway through his degree at Durham University, and on his debut in a one-day match against Warwickshire seconds at Edgbaston he scored 64 against a good attack and then made 98 in a Second XI Championship game against Kent before running himself out. We offered him a two-year summer contract and I think when he signed he thought he'd done the hard bit. When he turned up from university in June 1997 he was overweight and had clearly enjoyed the student lifestyle a bit too much.

On one of his first days back with us he twanged his hamstring in a sprint session and so after I spoke to Andy Wagner, who had been his coach at Radley College, I read him the Riot Act and he knuckled down. Andrew played a couple of one-day games that year and in 1998 made his Championship debut. When Justin Langer signed for Middlesex, he noticed Andrew's talent straightaway and took him under his wing a bit. Andrew never looked back after that.

The other player I vividly remember thinking had a special talent when I first saw him was Ed Joyce. Mike Hendrick, who coached Ireland at the time, recommended Ed and he turned up at RAF Vine Lane in 1999 and played against Sussex. We were short so I had to play in that match and when I saw him at the other end while we briefly batted together I thought I was watching David Gower again. He had so much time to play, possessed all the shots and a fantastic temperament. Ed wanted to be a professional cricketer and nothing was going to get in his way, he was totally focused with a talent and temperament to match. I rang Don Bennett that night to tell him I thought we had a good 'un and Don came to watch him score 150 against Lancashire seconds a few weeks later. Within a year he was a Middlesex regular and went on to have a fantastic career, as a batsman and later as captain at Sussex as well as playing for England and Ireland.

There were others. Owais Shah played in the second team aged 15 having already looked to the manner born when he took on Angus Fraser in the nets at Finchley while Gus was warming up for an England tour and bowling off 17 paces. Jason Pooley had the best hand-eye co-ordination of any player I have ever worked with. He should have played far more for Middlesex than he did but when the coach doesn't rate you it's going to be hard.

The coach in question was John Buchanan, who had a year in charge in 1998. He came with a big reputation having led Queensland to the first Sheffield Shield in their history and he quickly set about trying to make an impression. Mark Ramprakash, who was in his second year as captain, was on tour with England when we went to Portugal for a pre-season trip. John insisted on training runs at 5.30am and everyone bought into it, even if some of the players had only been in their beds for a couple of hours after a night out! John videoed every ball that summer, which was unheard of then, to help players overcome technical flaws he had spotted, and his preparation and net sessions were always interesting and innovative.

But there had always been clear demarcation lines at Middlesex as to what was the captain's responsibility and what was the coach's and Ramps felt John crossed those lines. Before the season started, having just returned from the Caribbean, Mark Ramprakash and the squad met with John and the rest of the staff at Finchley and Ramprakash blew his stack. It wasn't direct criticism aimed at John, but he was unhappy at the lack of honest communication from the club as to who was responsible for what.

Alan Moss, the chairman of cricket, had told Ramps that, as captain, he had to decide things like what the team wore, when they travelled to games and when they practised, which had always been the case during Mike Gatting's 14 years in charge. It turned out Moss had told Buchanan exactly the same while Ramps was in the West Indies with England. There is a funny story around this. A couple of weeks later, the players and I were sitting in the hotel bar in Manchester ahead of a 7pm team meeting before playing Lancashire, after travelling up from Canterbury during the day, when Buchanan called to say that he was still in Birmingham, stuck in traffic!

Mark rightly felt his authority was being undermined and, although he and John shook hands and agreed to get on with it as the season was only a few days away, we had a terrible year and finished 17th in the Championship, 12th in the Sunday League and were knocked out of both one-day competitions in the quarter-finals. At the end of the season to no one's great surprise John left and Mike Gatting, who had just retired after 24 seasons as a player, took over as director of coaching, having been told earlier that summer by Buchanan that he should not delay his retirement any longer.

Would I have taken the job had it been offered to me? Absolutely, but that never happened and I was a little pissed off not to be considered. With players like Gatt and Keith Brown retiring and others moving on the squad was in transition and no one knew the younger players and whether they could make the step up better than me. But Gatt was always going to be Middlesex coach once he'd retired as a player. He was, and I suppose still is, Mr Middlesex and he is the most loyal person I have come across in cricket. But I don't think Gatt was cut out to be a coach and appointing him at that time was a mistake. But Don Bennett, who was still on the committee and wielded a lot of influence after coaching the team for nearly 30 years, wanted him to take over and his views had a lot of clout.

The big problem as I saw it was that Gatt still thought of himself as one of the lads. He'd go out with the players for a beer on away trips and while I was the last person to criticise anyone for socialising I felt players used it as an excuse when they weren't picked. One minute they'd be at the bar with the coach, the next day he'd have to drop them and they would end up in my lap in the second team full of resentment. In 1999 our results only improved marginally and we finished 16th so found ourselves in Division Two when the Championship was split.

It was now that our decision earlier in the decade not to promote our own youngsters more vigorously came back to haunt us. Some left, others stayed but didn't fulfil their promise and we made stopgap signings like bringing back Mike Roseberry from Durham and taking on players like Robin Weston and Kevin Shine who, with no disrespect, were no better than the players we'd had a few years earlier and who had left the club. I thought Middlesex's ethos, which had always been to develop their own players, was being disregarded. At the time, Gatt and I fell out over it which made the last year or so of my time there a bit fraught, even though my job title was now club coach and I was working more with the first-team players.

Things didn't improve much on the pitch in 2000 so when I took a call from Vinny Codrington, the secretary, in late July to attend a meeting at Lord's I knew what was coming. What I didn't suspect was that when I turned up to get the sack Gatt would be leaving the Middlesex office in a right state while I was walking in. I'd never seen him so upset. It turned out he had been fired as well.

I accepted that my time was up. What I took exception to were the reasons given for my dismissal – that I hadn't been helping to produce players for the first team. Now justified criticism I could take but I felt that was complete bullshit. Phil Edmonds had been part of the panel that made the decision but in my opinion Phil didn't give two hoots about Middlesex the day he stopped playing for them. The sacking didn't hurt me but the reasons for it did and I still resent it to this day. I don't feel bitterness towards Middlesex as a club but I do towards Edmonds, who was on a massive ego trip on the committee and had little knowledge of the players or what was going on behind the scenes. I ended up staying until the end of the season, mainly because I needed the money, and the club were happy about this. But not surprisingly I lost interest and so did Gatt.

I thought he deserved a bit more time after just two years in the job. I did feel he was starting to make some progress, but they wanted a clean sweep. It was no surprise to me when they appointed Phil Edmonds's old sparring partner John Emburey as Mike's replacement. He'd gone into coaching at

Northamptonshire after retiring but hadn't been very successful. I felt shabbily treated and disrespected but that was that. My Middlesex career was over. What was I going to do next?

During my early years on the coaching staff I had occasionally helped Don Bennett out with the first team and in 1995 I was at Uxbridge assisting Don during a game against Northamptonshire when Alan Whitehead, one of the umpires, was taken ill. It was roasting hot and I think the heat had affected Alan, so I stood at square leg all day and rather enjoyed it. Over the next few years I did more stints when umpires failed to show for second-team matches, which happened quite often, and began to get even more of a taste for it. There was usually a senior umpire appointed to second-team matches so I would talk to guys like Allan Jones, David Constant, David Shepherd and Mervyn Kitchen, who all encouraged me to give full-time umpiring a go.

So when I left Middlesex at the end of 2000, I knew my only route back into the game was umpiring. I did all of the training courses and then was interviewed for the reserve panel. There were plenty of former players on the umpires' circuit but not many of them were in my age group or younger and the ECB recognised this. Even so, I had to work hard to convince the interview panel that I wanted the job because I thought I could do it well rather than because I needed something to do. It was still a surprise to be told I was in and I was delighted. I took my final exams the day after my mum died and spent the following winter talking through various on-field scenarios with umpires I knew at all levels of the game.

And so on 16 April 2001 at the Riverside ground in Chester-le-Street, I walked out with Neil Mallender to umpire my first first-class match – Durham versus Durham UCCE. There was snow in the air, the players all wore bobble hats because it was so cold, the wind seemed to be blowing directly from the Arctic and the students were dismissed for 67 in their first innings. Neil had kindly given me choice of ends before play started and I made the first wrong decision of my umpiring career by choosing to stand in the teeth of the freezing-cold gale-force easterly wind for the whole game. But I absolutely loved it. 'This is for me,' I told Neil at the end of the first day. And nearly 20 years later it still is.

11

On the Circuit

I KNEW pretty quickly that I had found my true vocation on a cricket field and although that first full season in 2001, after my debut at Durham, consisted mainly of second-team games, I loved it. I visited places I'd never heard of as well, which I quite liked doing: Pontarddulais, Barnt Green, Blackpool, Bournemouth and Banstead to name but a few. For a lot of the clubs, staging second-team matches was a big thing. You were always looked after and, as I discovered, the facilities were sometimes better than at some of the first-class county grounds.

I didn't join the international circuit for another five years, but it wasn't long into my first full season when I had an unexpected opportunity which convinced me that I wanted to be more than just a county umpire. I was doing a second-team friendly between Kent and Essex at Folkestone when I took a call from Andy Smith, who looked after the umpires in those days for the ECB. Would I mind going to Chelmsford to do a first-class game?

'No problem, who is it against?'

'Australia.'

It's a good job I'd pulled over on the M2 to take the call otherwise I'd have probably crashed the car. Andy insisted that he hadn't called me because they had no one else. 'We want you to do the game because we think you're good enough,' he said. I hardly slept at all that night, my mind racing with all sorts of possibilities. I knew that Australia would play a strong side as it was their last warm-up game before the first Test at Edgbaston, but I wasn't sure if I was ready for the step up. I have never been more nervous before or since, even when I made my various debuts for Middlesex, Sussex and even England.

My biggest concern wasn't the game itself, but how Australia coach John Buchanan would behave towards me. I had never found out if John thought I had anything to do with Middlesex's decision to let him go as coach a few years earlier. I hadn't – it was a decision made by the committee – but when we met on the first day at Chelmsford he was brilliant and didn't even mention Middlesex. And after the game he was complimentary about my performance. Not for the first time in my life, I'd misjudged someone.

The first Australian I met at Chelmsford was Justin Langer, an erstwhile colleague at Middlesex. After expressing his surprise that I'd taken up umpiring he introduced me to the players, a few of whom I knew from the circuit anyway. And in the Essex team there were a lot of people – Nasser Hussain, Ronnie Irani, Paul Grayson and Peter Such – that I'd known for years. Australia played a strong side – only Steve Waugh and Shane Warne weren't involved – and umpiring while guys like Glenn McGrath, Jason Gillespie and Brett Lee came steaming in, or watching batsmen like Damien Martyn and Adam Gilchrist make it look so easy was a real thrill. It was clearly a step up from second-team cricket at Folkestone, that's for sure, and I concentrated fiercely. But occasionally, during drinks breaks, I did allow my mind to wander a bit. Imagine doing this all the time, watching the best players in the world?

The game petered out into a boring draw after Australia batted through the third and final day to get some practice in. The ground was still packed, as it had been for the first two days, and Ronnie Irani, who was captaining Essex, decided to entertain the crowd after tea by putting on the pads and letting James Foster, who had been keeping wicket, bowl a couple of overs. All harmless fun, or so I thought until an hour or so after the game had finished.

It had been a draining three days but after ringing Jo to tell her how well I thought it had gone I was sitting in the dressing room feeling pretty pleased with myself when the door almost came off its hinges and Ronnie Irani burst through, followed not long afterwards by Nasser Hussain.

'What the fuck, Gunner? Why have you reported us to Lord's?'

I didn't have a clue what they were talking about until Ronnie told me that the umpires had filed a complaint to ECB through Essex's chief executive David East stating that, by bowling Foster, Essex had brought the game into disrepute. This was all news to me. I sent them to see David and bring back the report which they did. It turned out that my fellow umpire Trevor Jesty had indeed reported Essex, but without telling me and certainly without getting my signature on the charge sheet. In the space of an hour or so I went from being as high as a kite to a feeling of utter disappointment. For the next 48 hours or so I tried to call Trevor but he never got back to me. We've umpired together many times since and I have never brought up what happened at Chelmsford, although he knew the extent of my feelings by speaking to other umpires. What was the point? But it taught me a valuable lesson about umpires working as a partnership.

That night I sat down and wrote loads of notes about the three days, what I'd done right, what I'd done wrong and what I enjoyed the most. I realised that in terms of the basics I was a good umpire. I knew the laws, my basic decision-making was sound and I was already getting a reputation on the circuit as a players' umpire – someone who had been there and knew about the ups and downs of the game. Physically I was fine. Even when I was coaching Middlesex I used to enjoy training with the players and when I wasn't umpiring I would be outside cutting grass or rolling cricket wickets. But I knew I still had a few rough edges.

In those first couple of years on the circuit I greatly relied on the advice of an umpire I knew from Berkshire called Dave Burden. He was a terrific umpire locally, who would take four or five weeks off in the summer just so he could stand in as many games as he could from schools' matches to MCC games. He was very well respected and could easily have been a first-class umpire if he'd wanted to be. Dave would come and watch me at all sorts of places in those first couple of years. I sometimes spotted him in the crowd, which wasn't difficult at most second-team games as hardly anyone showed up, but often he would slip in unnoticed and observe my demeanour on the field.

The first bit of advice he gave me was to change my headgear. I'd taken to wearing a pork pie hat similar to that worn by Sid James in the *Carry On* films. I liked it but it probably didn't give off a very professional impression of me. So one afternoon Dave pointed me in the direction of a company called Panama Jack and I wore their hats for the next few years. Dave advised me on my general persona on the field: how I stood, even the way I raised my finger when I gave people out. He could see that I enjoyed the craic with the players, but he told me to tone it down a bit, to refine my personality.

I learned some important lessons from Dave. How could I banter with the players one minute, then give them out the next? More than once in those formative years I was buttonholed by a player I'd given out whom I'd earlier shared a laugh or two with on the field. 'I thought we were mates?' I was told more than once. By the time I was regularly on the first-class list in 2002 the word on the circuit was that while I liked a bit of fun, I was a stickler for good behaviour. Players knew that if they crossed that line with me they would be in the umpires' room at the end of play. I never did the job to be praised, although I was grateful for the encouragement of people like Peter Moores, the former England coach, in my early days when he was in charge at Sussex and for the fact that, if I did fall down a hole, my colleague on the field would grab me. That hasn't always been the case among domestic umpires over the years.

Back then there was still a strong group of senior guys on the circuit, some of whom had been at it for nearly 20 years. Almost to a man, I found them unfailingly helpful and supportive. I was still playing when some of them first started umpiring but blokes like Mervyn Kitchen, David Constant, Vanburn Holder, George Sharp, Barrie Leadbeater, Alan Whitehead, Ray Julian and Barry Dudleston – who mentored me for a while when I got on the international panel in 2006 – were all terrific with me. They were characters in their own way. Alan had a bit of a reputation for being hard work, but we hit it off over a shared love of the nags. Umpires have to be at a ground two hours before the start of play which is a lot of downtime so Alan and I would often work out our Yankee for the day over a cup of coffee.

I must have driven some of these guys nuts with my constant questions about this law or that, what this regulation meant and even how to work out Duckworth-Lewis. I was never frightened to ask and they were always ready to help. As well as the day-to-day umpiring I didn't mind the travelling either in those days, but you could see why some of the older guys lost their spark. It wore down the best of them, sometimes due to ridiculous scheduling. I remember David Constant coming to Harrow to do Middlesex seconds the day after he'd umpired in a five-day Test at Lord's. How was he expected to be at his sharpest for the next three days after the physical and mental strain of umpiring a Test match? Most first-class umpires had to do the occasional second-team match and when I was Middlesex coach I never marked them down, even if they'd had a bad game, because I could see how hard it was for them to adjust to coming down to umpire at that level.

As well as the senior guys there was also a new generation coming through, people like Mark Benson,

Jeremy Lloyds and Neil Bainton. Neil hadn't played the first-class game and spent his off-season delivering the post in Essex, but he was and still is an outstanding umpire. No one knows the laws better than Neil, and I frequently consulted him during the next 20 years. Because he doesn't do the job all year round, when he comes back to it in the summer he is refreshed and clear-headed. He is still one of our best umpires.

It was only some years later that ECB introduced a points system for player indiscretions on the field. For many years, anyone who crossed the line would come to the umpires' room after play for a verbal dressing down and usually, after an apology and a handshake, we'd move on. There were a lot more journalists at county games in those days and they normally found out if players had stepped out of line. If I was ever approached by a reporter I would always tell them what had happened, in the expectation that if it appeared in the paper it might embarrass the player into behaving himself in future.

There is no doubt in my mind that player behaviour in the county game has steadily declined over the years. The days when umpires could have a quiet word with a player or captain and the game would carry on have all but disappeared. With two divisions in the County Championship there is a lot more at stake, and there are also massive rewards for reaching the big showpiece occasions like Twenty20 Finals Day. Players are well paid, certainly in relation to what I earned, and with that comes more expectation to perform.

Players have always pushed the boundaries to see what they could get away with, but it has got worse, even more so in the last few years when the all-seeing eye of social media has given everyone a platform and players find themselves under more scrutiny than ever from the outside, often by people who aren't even at the game. A player has a couple of bad scores and his or his county's Twitter page is inundated with comments criticising him and telling him he can't play the game. It's the same for us umpires. I don't use social media, but someone told me a couple of years ago that there is a Facebook group with quite a few members in the subcontinent calling for me to be sacked as an international umpire!

I have made more than my fair share of howlers but, unlike some of my more intransigent colleagues over the years, I have never been afraid to admit it. If I apologise to a player whom I've given out wrongly at the end of a day's play I always feel better, even if he or she doesn't. I remember giving Durham's Phil Mustard out in my first Lord's final in 2007 between Durham and Hampshire when Phil was going well, and I decided he was lbw to a ball from James Bruce which was going so far down the leg side it probably wouldn't have hit another set. I apologised to Phil and fortunately Durham won the game easily but every time I saw him after that he always mentioned that I'd spoiled his opportunity to score a hundred in a Lord's final! Players do hold grudges against certain umpires and, on many occasions, I have had to speak to those who have been given out by my colleague and explain that actually he is good at his job and that he should be cut some slack as we often do with the players.

As more players arrived from overseas, where a lot of the umpires they encountered in their domestic cricket were part-time and they could get away with a lot more, behaviour got worse. Some of the players learned the hard way that what was acceptable back home wouldn't be tolerated in England. There perhaps aren't the strong characters these days that there were 20 years or so ago. England players turned out for their counties a bit more than they do now and they would invariably be targeted by the opposition's overseas star. I remember a proper verbal bust-up involving Hampshire's Shane Warne, Sussex captain Chris Adams and Matt Prior, who had just broken through at international level. Adams and Prior tried to take Warne on with some verbals but Warne, as he so often did, had the last word when he got Matt out and gave him a proper send-off.

County cricket can be a hard school for young players, no matter their reputation or ability, and if I sometimes gave the benefit of the doubt to the senior man I made no apology for it. Even someone like Warne knew when he'd overstepped the mark but often it took incidents like that to make sure young players pulled their horns in a bit and learned when it was time to get their head down and show a bit of respect to senior pros.

I'd barely got into my umpiring stride when Twenty20 started in 2003. I remember standing in the pilot game in Bristol and wondering if it had much of a future. I was all for 20 overs having to be bowled in 1 hour and 15 minutes, although that day Shoaib Akhtar took 15 minutes to bowl the first over after sending down four no-balls and three wides! The authorities were seriously thinking about introducing a golden over, with the captain literally pulling a golden ticket from his back pocket at the start of the over when all runs scored would be doubled. That didn't get beyond the pilot stage, but the format soon captured the public's imagination. I remember turning up to umpire games in that first summer at grounds that I had never seen a quarter full, even for big one-day games, that were suddenly packed to the rafters. Now, there were women and families watching and the product itself was fantastic. I did Finals Day for the first time in 2009 and because I wasn't umpiring England internationals at home very much at that stage of my career I loved the experience at Edgbaston, the colour and noise from the crowd, even if for a lot of them what's going on in the middle is secondary to what's happening in the stands. I haven't done Finals Day since because ECB want to give their younger umpires a taste of the experience of those big occasions and I think that's the right thing to do.

Twenty20 has gone from strength to strength in every aspect except one: the quality of the pitches. In the last few years I can't believe how many really poor wickets have been prepared, especially at the end of the group stages. I totally appreciate that it's hard work for groundsmen, particularly at grounds with smaller squares, to provide new pitches for every game but sometimes I think they feel that it doesn't matter what surface they provide because people will come and watch regardless and the quality of the wicket will soon be forgotten. They might be right – but it doesn't mean it's the correct thing to do.

At Twenty20, people want to see the ball flying out of the ground or into the stands, they don't want some dibbly-dobbly merchant bowling four overs and taking 1-10 on a slow, low shit-heap. They are being short-changed and it doesn't sit right with me. It will probably get worse with the advent of The Hundred in 2020 and the extra demands that the new competition places on county groundstaff. Hybrid pitches, which offer a mix of real and artificial grass, are surely the way forward in the long term. I know they are expensive, but if the curse of poor pitches cannot be solved the spectacle itself will be diluted and people will eventually be put off from watching.

Like players, umpires have their favourite grounds as well. I never say this too loudly when I'm in Sussex or Middlesex, but I have always loved going to the Oval. I have had bad games, but I have never not wanted to work there. The room we have is fantastic and most importantly the bounce is consistent. Give an umpire a pitch with even bounce, wherever it is in the world, and he will be happy. Cardiff, which is not everyone's cup of tea, is another favourite place to visit. I didn't umpire my first Sussex game at Hove until September 2002 and it took me until 2006 before I stood in a Middlesex Championship match for the first time at Lord's but there was never any question of favouritism towards my old counties. In fact, I have occasionally been accused of giving too many decisions in favour of their opponents!

My routine has always been the same. I get to the ground a couple of hours before, go out to the middle and discuss the weather and the pitch with the groundsman, put my gear on and then sit in our room and try to take my mind off the game, which for me normally involves putting on a bet, having my last fag until lunchtime and drinking a couple of cups of coffee. At lunch, I have seen umpires demolish three-course meals and go back for seconds. I prefer a sandwich or a salad. And another cigarette of course. After a shower at the end of play I will normally have a pint or two with my umpiring colleague but these days I am more often back in the hotel and in bed by 9pm.

In 2020 I will be starting my 19th year on the domestic circuit and it will be probably be my biggest challenge since my first season on the first-class list. Since 2006 I have had only limited exposure to county cricket but during that time the ECB have been wonderfully supportive and accommodating when I have been in England to work. I know the governing body come in for criticism now and again, but I cannot speak highly enough of them as an employer. I remember at the pre-season umpires' meeting a couple of years ago a colleague who I won't name complained about the allowances we get which I thought was ridiculous and I stood up and told him and everyone else so. It is not a life-changing sum, but we are paid well, so well that you could live off what you earn from March to September for the rest of the year. I think of people I know still doing the 9 to 5 on the Slough Trading Estate with only five weeks off a year and thank my lucky stars for the opportunities I've had.

When I had my breakdown, Chris Kelly, who looks after the umpires, was one of the first people to contact me and was wonderfully supportive when I eased my way back. It's a good life with a good pension and I owe it to ECB as much as anyone to commit to a season in England in 2020. It is something I am looking forward to. I want to maintain my personal standards, to be able to walk off the field at the end of a day's play with the same satisfaction as I had in 2001 and during all the years since. I don't doubt that

I still have the ability to umpire well but the appeal of getting in the car and driving all over the country has slowly lost its appeal.

Peak time is going to be August when we will have had Twenty20, The Hundred will have just begun and the 50-over competition will be starting. Now I am the first to admit that umpiring for 40 overs is not that physically onerous but the almost daily travelling at peak times of the season is. If I am still enjoying it by that stage of the summer I will probably continue for 2021 and maybe beyond but I can't see me still going strong at the retirement age for domestic umpires of 65. There are younger guys who need opportunities and I will be the first to say if I feel my own standards have slipped while there are enough people who will tell me when it's time, one of them being Jo. I won't drag my heels.

I have lost count of the times over the last 20 years or so when, as I head towards Old Trafford or Headingley, someone like Richard Kettleborough, who lives in Sheffield, is packing his bag and driving to Sussex. In 20 years or so I have never fallen asleep at the wheel or had an accident caused by tiredness but quite a few of my colleagues have. My car did break down on the way to Derby in 2019 and Chris Kelly had to get David Millns to stand in for me at short notice. I was actually disappointed. I hadn't been to Derby for 12 years and I was looking forward to seeing how much the place had improved.

I can definitely see burnout among umpires becoming an issue in the future. What's the answer? Regionalising appointments is the obvious one. Now, even someone like me would get bored of walking to Hove every day to umpire but there are plenty of grounds in the south-east which aren't more than 90 minutes away by car including Southampton, Chelmsford and Canterbury as well as the two London venues at the Oval and Lord's. Believe me, most umpires are more concerned about how long it's going to take to get somewhere than the teams they are working with. It wasn't until the end of the 2019 season, when I did a few domestic games following my retirement from the ICC panel, that I realised I'd umpired Hampshire and Surrey three times each in those few weeks but I hadn't even noticed. For us, it's still the same. Two sets of stumps 22 yards away and 22 players. Let's get on with it.

By August most umpires are tired and obviously the older you get the harder it becomes physically to keep going and performing, if that's the right description for an umpire, at a consistently high standard. Not so long ago during the county season you could guarantee there would be a few days when play would not be possible because of rain and you could have a breather but the drainage at most grounds now is superb and it's very rare that a day's play anywhere is called off before lunch. I always carry a set of golf clubs in the boot for that eventuality and, of course, a copy of *Coral's Racing Diary*. If there's a meeting on within striking distance I will go there. Mind you, I'm not sure Hexham is really within striking distance of Old Trafford but I did go there, as I'd never been before, for an evening meeting once after a washout in Manchester and had a lovely time at another of our many picturesque National Hunt courses.

DRS has made life a lot different for the international umpire and with the technology around there might come a day when it's used in domestic cricket as well. It's a potential issue, and another personal fear is the proliferation of tournaments around the world now, particularly T10 and T20 leagues. These are very attractive short-term tournaments for players – and umpires. If you can make enough money working at these for a few weeks of the year, is there any need for the foot-slog of the county circuit?

Similarly, will former players like me be as keen to become umpires in future when regular slots in one or two of the franchise leagues help pay off the mortgage? But my biggest concern is the amount of cricket being played these days around the world. I turn on the TV even in the depths of winter these days and there seems to be a game on somewhere in the world where quite a few of the participants, and even the umpires, are familiar faces. I think it's too much. Eventually the best players will fall down because they play too much. Their welfare has to be paramount. Without them, there is no game.

12

What's Next?

AS the new decade began, the ICC gave the green light to something which I think could mean the end of elite panel umpiring.

I'm talking about the decision – which had been endorsed by the international umpires in 2019 – to allow the third umpire to adjudicate on all front foot no-ball calls, not the on-field blokes. It was due to be used for the first time at the women's T20 World Cup in Australia in February and March 2020. I remember it being discussed at one of the last ICC meetings I attended before stepping down. Geoff Allardice, ICC's General Manager for Cricket, warned that if it was accepted, for umpires it would be like turkeys voting for Christmas. He's right and

I think within a couple of years there will be no need for elite umpires.

If you think about it, what is left for an international umpire to do now? DRS has completely changed the way Test and one-day matches are umpired since it was introduced and the technology that is used is only going to get better in the future, not scaled back. Now, umpires might not even need to worry about checking the front foot any more either because someone is doing that for them. Run outs can also be referred 'upstairs' of course. So what's left? I'm sure one of the TV production crew members is quite capable of putting the bails on the stumps before the start of play. I suppose the boys could go out there and count to six before calling over, but there is surely technology that can do that simple task as well and save umpires the bother.

Why send umpires all over the world at tremendous expense to the ICC when, with all the technology now available, they might as well stay at home and umpire in matches in their own countries if they have relatively little to do any more? I'm sure someone like Richard Kettleborough or Richard Illingworth would love to stand in an Ashes Test at Lord's, alongside Bruce Oxenford, the Australian umpire, who would be just as chuffed. Just take umpires' calls out of the equation and get DRS to clarify every decision. It will have one benefit: the best umpires will stand in the most high-profile series involving the big three: England, Australia and India. The only thing technology can't handle is the management of the players themselves. Which is something I am pretty good at.

Why didn't the guys kick up a fuss about this? Well, it is one less thing for them to worry about and most don't even look at the front line when a bowler lands his foot anyway. I always did, and I used to get pissed off with colleagues who didn't. Most of them shrugged their shoulders, denied that they had not, and we moved on.

When I reflect on my time on the international panel, there have been some pretty seismic changes during those 13 years. I remember going to South Africa, at ICC's behest, in 2007 when all the ICC umpires were invited to watch the T20 World Cup Final between India and Pakistan, which was very pleasant. Mark Benson and Simon Taufel were in charge and I was more than a little jealous as they walked out to umpire the game. Actually, it inspired me.

Something less than inspiring was the three-day umpires' seminar which started the following day. It was at this first seminar I attended that I met Steve Davis, who became a great friend on and off the field over the next few years. I have been to many more of these seminars since and the best part is always the opportunity to socialise with the other guys, some of whom you hardly see from one year to the next.

The meetings themselves can be mind-numbingly boring but the first one was a bit of an eye-opener. There must have been nearly 40 of us there from the top umpires like Simon, Billy Bowden and Steve Bucknor, who was in his last season on the elite panel, down to newbies like me and Nigel Llong. On the second morning, the 12 elite umpires went off into another room for a meeting, leaving the rest of us to twiddle our thumbs for two days. We just hung around, learned absolutely jack shit and then went out in the evening and enjoyed ourselves. When I got back to London, Chris Kelly asked to see Nigel Llong, who had travelled out there with me, and I for feedback. He couldn't believe ECB had forked out to send us halfway around the world for what was effectively a jolly and a complete waste of their money and, if truth be told, our time.

When we did mingle, it became apparent there were some big egos at work, a bit like a cricket dressing room really, which didn't surprise me. But I sensed that the elite guys – men like Steve Bucknor, Daryl Harper, Simon Taufel and Billy Bowden – felt a little threatened by the newcomers and, if I'd been in their position, I would have probably thought the same. That was why they went into conclave on their own. When we met again a year later it was pretty much the same deal and, over the subsequent years and seminars I have attended, always at great cost to ICC, I can't say I learned a great deal at all. We had some fun in the evenings but that wasn't the point.

But I kept my mouth shut, learned what I could and got on with it but, before I made my debut in the England v Sri Lanka one-day international at the Oval later in 2006, I spent much of the build-up skimming through the ICC regulations to make sure I was sort of up to speed. You had to think on your feet – there was no third-umpire simulations or training in procedure and protocol. Of course you were expected to know the laws, which I did, but you soon learned you had to rely on your usually more experienced partner for any on-the-job training. In that regard I was so lucky that Darrell Hair, whom I stood with, was one of the best and there weren't too many scenarios he hadn't experienced. The English umpires had been well trained by ECB, but I felt sorry for some of the other lads who were new to the international scene like me. For them it was sink or swim such was the lack of support they got from their authorities back home.

You have to remember that back then the respective boards of control effectively ran the ICC. The chief executive at the time was Malcolm Speed, who was a great guy and a very good administrator, but a lot of what went on behind the scenes there seemed a bit amateurish to me, especially compared to what I was used to with ECB.

As general manager, David Richardson was in charge of cricket operations at the time, after he was appointed in 2002 and, for ten years, he did a good job and was a fine bloke, but Doug Cowie who was appointed umpires' manager in 2006 was, in my opinion, out of his depth.

Doug had been a fine umpire and had only recently retired, but the game moved on so quickly and he struggled to keep up. I remember at one meeting in Dubai, Doug trying to explain the primitive machinations of DRS and David Richardson having to step in so he could finish the lecture because Doug was floundering a bit.

I had been an international umpire for ten years before I got my first 'coach' as such when Denis Burns began working for me in 2016. Denis has been brilliant to me and our friendship will endure long after I have given up umpiring for good. I can't thank him enough for what he's done for me, particularly during my breakdown after the incident during the World Cup in 2015 in Australia. I only wish he'd been on the scene earlier as a sounding board – someone you could talk to and feed back to – because, in those early days, your chances of becoming an elite panel member largely depended on the marks you got from match referees after each match.

Your relationship with the referee was more important than with any of the players, which I thought was wrong. Basically, if you knew where your bread was buttered you had to suck up to them. If they wanted a red wine at the hotel bar in the evening, you got them a red wine.

I remember doing a one-day international between England and India when I was TV umpire. I nipped off to the gents and came back to find my glasses had disappeared. The referee had hidden them as a joke and sat there while I frantically searched through my bags trying to find them. I had my suspicions he'd hidden them and decided to walk out and leave him and the others to it. It was only when I started to pack my bag that he sheepishly handed them back.

Like umpires, match referees should have a shelf life as well, but you can see why they want to cling on to the job because it's a great life. All expenses paid, going around the world and if the game passes off without incident, which the vast majority still do, a very relaxing few days, especially now that DRS is helping umpires to get decisions right so there are fewer flashpoints on the field which can't be handled with some good man management by the umpires.

There are some very good match referees. Jeff Crowe and Alan Hurst were excellent because they cared about the game. Andy Pycroft, Javagal Srinath and David Boon are good as well because they have your back. Everyone who comes across him loves Boony, and his biggest asset is that he is passionate about cricket and about upholding standards. He's not bothered about upsetting people or worried about where we're all going to dinner that night. He's brilliant at his job and the common denominator with him and the others I have mentioned is that they are relatively recent ex-players. Modern players have far more respect for you if they know you've played at the highest level, as I discovered during the early part of my career.

But sitting next to some referees for seven hours a day and then being expected to socialise in the evening as well is hard work, especially because you know that if you don't play the game they can mark you down. In my early years, there were several occasions when I refused to go out with the rest of the umpiring team the night before a match because I wanted to concentrate on my own preparation, which tended to involve a couple of quiet beers and an early night. The last thing I wanted to do was to go to dinner and talk about cricket for hours on end. Eventually, colleagues realised I wasn't being difficult, it was just the way I got ready to do my job.

But I knew I was taking a risk by adopting that stance and that I'd be accused of not being part of the team and even being anti-social, which I found very hard to accept. In one report, my on-field performance was rated as outstanding, but the match referee marked me down because I hadn't gone for a curry with the other umpires the night before the match started. Seriously, that's what it said.

On another occasion I got similarly good feedback for my performance on the field but was marked down because the referee felt I smoked too much! As my own profile grew and I started to be respected for who I was and the job I did, it soon became obvious why there was this antagonism towards me – plain and simple jealousy, of my reputation as someone the players liked and enjoyed being umpired by. I'd come into it with the intention of being different, of being someone who wanted to umpire in the way I'd have liked to have been when I played and I have always tried to be true to my word.

I remember doing a series in the West Indies with Richard Illingworth. One of the matches finished early and our flight out to the next venue wasn't until late the next day so we spent the day on the beach in Barbados and the referee came with us and worked on his report. He flew home and the next day Illy came to see me in a right state. 'Fucking look at this,' he said as he thrust the report in my hand. The referee had ticked the box saying he'd spoken to Richard about his performance when he hadn't, even though they had spent most of the previous day sitting next to each other on the beach! Priceless. Richard later told me it was the lowest point of his umpiring career, but he took it up with ICC and the referee rightly was taken to task.

In my first couple of years I couldn't stand the bullying and the bullshit and seriously considered jacking it in altogether in 2007 and going back to the day job with the ECB in county cricket. I told Chris Kelly, Doug Cowie and David Richardson and they were all very supportive and urged me to reconsider and eventually I did.

I made one decision then though – I never read another match referee's report. From then on for the next 12 years I could have had the best feedback ever, but I wouldn't have known about it. When the emails used to come through, I'd delete them without giving them a second thought. If I was doing something wrong during a match, I was honest enough to admit it and, if necessary, apologise for it. And if I ever needing convincing either way on a decision, there was always a 90ft-sized replay screen in the ground for reassurance – or otherwise!

After that I felt better about myself and I also began to appreciate the views of people in and around the game that I respected when they told me to calm down occasionally or gave me some advice. I have already mentioned the late Peter Roebuck, but another was the great Sri Lanka batsman Kumar Sangakkara, who didn't say a great deal but was always great with me. I never felt I overstepped the mark in terms of my relationship with players. I knew when the line was about to be crossed and could pull myself back, but occasionally I had to be reminded of that.

By 2008 I was at peace with myself but for other umpires the bullying and bullshit was harder for them to escape. I have umpired many times with guys who are literally scared of making a mistake, for fear of the repercussions for their career. You can't have that. Umpiring is not an exact science. We're all human so we all make mistakes. I was lucky, because I had a fallback position and a job with ECB, but for a lot of the others there was no structure in their own countries in which they could earn a living from umpiring full-time.

If I'd read the match reports, I might not have been so surprised when I took a call from Dave Richardson while I was sitting on a wall outside a hotel in Hamilton having a quiet smoke. I was there with Simon Taufel umpiring in what was only my third Test match between New Zealand and India.

When you saw Dave's name on your phone you didn't know what to expect.

'Morning Gunner, how are you? Look, I'm not going to beat about the bush. Would you like to become an elite umpire?'

I didn't fall off the wall, but I did take a very big drag on my cigarette. It was one of the happiest moments of my life and my biggest achievement in the game without a doubt. I played for England, but there was a lot of luck involved in my selection. This felt so much better. It was also a bit of a shock. Because I wasn't monitoring match reports any more, I didn't even know that captain's remarks were now being taken into consideration as well in assessing your performance. The timing was a little fortunate for me too because both Neil Mallender and Jeremy Lloyds had just come off the international list and there was a shortage of English umpires at the top level.

Because of the time difference I had to keep it quiet for a few hours before I could call Jo. I thought it was a big secret until Simon came up to me in the hotel lobby and offered his congratulations. I had a few drinks and a round of golf in the afternoon to celebrate and then I called Jo, who quickly brought me back down to earth. 'Well done,' she said. 'But

I've got to go because the kids need to get ready for school!'

When I got back to England, I had lunch with Chris Kelly. 'You know they are going to have a different opinion of you now, don't you?' was his abrupt warning. 'You are now regarded as one of the best umpires in the world and you will be under a lot more scrutiny.' I didn't think much would change, but when I went to Sri Lanka for my next series three months later, I have never been more nervous. I was in charge now. The rest of the umpiring team I was working with were looking to me for guidance and, where necessary, encouragement. Initially that was difficult, but I tried to remain true to myself. I did change because I had to act a bit more responsibly and show signs of leadership but I settled into the new role quite easily in the end.

I got another shock a few months later when Simon Taufel, who was effectively the shop steward for the elite umpires back then, called me into his hotel room near Lord's after I'd stood in a one-day international there against Australia. Up until then I hadn't given a thought to how much more I would be paid until he showed me my contract, which would run initially for 12 months as it was my first year on the elite panel. While Simon was going through the small print, I couldn't take my eyes off the figure at the bottom of the page. I was getting an eye-popping pay rise. I was shaking so much it was nearly ten minutes before I was composed enough to sign the contract.

I walked out of the hotel and strolled down towards Little Venice, sat on a bench and starting crying. Jo rang me and knew something was up but I didn't want to tell her over the phone so I asked her to come up to London the next day and we met in a pub called the Warwick Castle, where I often had a drink when I played or umpired at Lord's. When I showed her the contract she burst into tears as well.

Look, when I played and then when I became a coach, I earned decent money but never life-changing amounts. This was. For two young kids from Slough it was big news. Wow. I've never been much of a spender, but Jo can spend money, and she won't deny that. She had been through a lot, scrimping and saving when I was gallivanting around the world, so it was nice for her to be able to do things now without worrying about the cost and for us to help the kids buy things like cars or get on the property ladder. We took the decision to invest in property and that turned out to be a very sensible move. The grass-cutting business was going really well at that stage too and with the extra income from that we were able to move back to Sussex, which was something we'd always wanted to do but couldn't afford to do until then.

After that initial shock, the money I earned didn't bother me. I certainly never walked on to the field thinking how well I was getting paid or anything like that. On overseas trips I hardly ever had to spend a penny, because everything was paid for: travel, hotels, meals. It was a great life – I can't deny that – and I was very fortunate to enjoy it for 13 years.

Back to the ICC. Have all the decisions during my time been in the best interests of the game? Probably not. When DRS was introduced, I never felt we got the whole picture, certainly in terms of how they felt the system would develop over the years and how it would impact on umpires and their jobs. It was crazy, for example, that early on after its introduction we would go from one series which had DRS to another which didn't. It's a lot more uniform now of course, but I always thought it should have been brought in across the board, in all series, at the same time, no matter how long it might take. It was as if they had a new toy and couldn't wait to play with it. The broadcasters undoubtedly put them under pressure to bring it in as soon as they could.

DRS is here to stay, and no one can deny that, but in future I believe any improvements must be trialled properly before ICC enforce them. In the past they have often gone on a whim, in my opinion to suit the TV companies. For me, the biggest positive breakthrough was when they decided 'live to air' would be available to people in the ground as well as those watching at home, so everyone could hear the conversations between umpires on the field and third umpires when adjudicating on DRS reviews and expressions like 'let's rock and roll' entered cricket's dictionary. My biggest issue when that came in was trying to moderate my language when I had to get in touch with the third umpire because a player was questioning my call on an lbw decision!

I believed that a big error of judgement by ICC was the introduction of two balls in an innings in a one-day international. Before then, it was wonderful to watch the way certain bowlers could manipulate that white ball, particularly towards the end of an innings if they started to get it to reverse swing. Bowlers like Lasith Malinga and James Anderson were magicians at that. Now, one-day cricket is far too heavily weighted in the batsmen's favour. Because technology has improved in terms of how wickets are prepared and squares are covered so well, you tend to get a lot of flat wickets with a ball that does nothing being smashed around for 25 overs. Look, everyone loves to see the power generated by batsmen these days and the distances they hit a cricket ball are amazing but it's no longer a fair contest. A game where 350 plays 345 all the time makes for pretty dull cricket if you ask me.

When ICC make their recommendations, they have to be ratified by the World Cricket committee, which comes under the jurisdiction of MCC. Now there are some wonderful cricketers, past and present, on that committee but when they put a tie on, I sometimes get the feeling it strangles the oxygen to some of the best cricket brains in the world. Richard Kettleborough is in the invidious position of representing the umpires on the committee and I think it's very hard for him because while his opinion will be listened to and probably even respected he is never going to be able to change the majority view.

What has worked? The unanimity among the respective cricket boards to stamp out illegal bowling actions is one positive development. I remember in my early years when nine players were reported for a suspect action in the space of a month, now it's very rare. The boards went to the ICC and our bosses then told us umpires to nail them.

In terms of ball-tampering, all the time the game is played people will try to get away with it. One of the benefits of saturation coverage, and these days the all-seeing eye of social media as well, is that at international level it's a lot harder to go undetected because of the scrutiny each game is played under. But when it does take place, you have to nail the culprits and I think, by and large, that has happened. It's very hard for umpires to spot it themselves, even though we are thrown the ball at the end of every over, because it always goes on behind our backs and players are very clever at how they do it. You would be surprised how the application of a bit of spit and a rigorous polish can make marks on the ball's leather disappear for the few seconds it takes for an umpire to have a cursory inspection at the end of an over and throw it back to the bowler before the ball dries out and the marks and indentations can be worked on again.

Sometimes, though, you have to take action which is not strictly playing by the rules but gets the job done. During a one-day international I did early in my career I was convinced one of the teams were tampering with the ball so during one of the drinks breaks I nipped off and got a ladies' ball gauge out of my bag and stuck it in my pocket. My fellow umpire did not agree with what I was going to do but I thought 'fuck it'.

I was given the ball and it wouldn't fit through the ladies' gauge, so the ball was changed, and the same thing happened again after 26 overs. Unconventional and certainly not something ICC would necessarily agree with, but it stopped the team from getting away with sharp practice that day.

A few months after my retirement in June 2019, I got a call from ICC. Would I like to go to the Under-19 World Cup in South Africa at the start of 2020 and mentor the umpires, many of whom were standing in an international tournament for the first time? I didn't take long to agree because I had always hoped that ICC might use someone with my experience in this way – and a month in the sun during one of our wet winters was another attraction. As I have mentioned, when I started, umpiring was sink or swim – you were largely left to your own devices – so I know from my own experiences how daunting it could be coming into that environment for the first time. The Under-19

World Cup is a good place for the next generation to start. There was TV coverage but it's not the biggest event on the calendar.

Then, a couple of weeks before I was due to fly out with Denis Burns, a package arrived at home and inside was a couple of sets of umpiring kit for the tournament! I was surprised, because actually standing in games was never mentioned and my immediate thought was to say no. But I mulled it over for a few days and decided that I would do a few games. I hadn't done any umpiring since the end of the English domestic summer in 2019 and with the 2020 season not too far away I thought it would be an opportunity to get back into the swing of things. I ended up doing five matches.

Before the first of them I was actually pretty nervous. It had been one of the longest periods of inactivity in my career and I wondered if I still had it. I had heard on the grapevine that there weren't many good umpires coming through the system, but from what I saw in five weeks in South Africa that was bullshit. In particular, let me mark your card about Roly Black, an Irish umpire who is outstanding. If he doesn't make it all the way to the top, I will be amazed. And there are four or five others who are just as good and could easily make the step up when they get the chance. Whether they have the career I had remains to be seen. But I loved talking to them and finding out about them as people and what made them tick. We would sit on the bus on the way back to the hotel from a game and I'd ask them to write down three things which they had got out of that day's game and see if they were the same as I had put for them. Mostly they were.

It's no use me trying to do that when I'm umpiring alongside them because I've got my own performance to worry about. But mentoring umpires is something I would love to do in the future, as much to act as an ice breaker when they meet players, groundsmen, TV people or whoever for the first time. I know how daunting that can be from the experiences I had at the start of my career. It was slightly easier for me because I'd been a player and coach, so for guys like Roly, who has no great profile in cricket, that could potentially be awkward. I can't tell people how to umpire like me, Simon Taufel or Richard Kettleborough. You probably need a bit of all three of us to succeed in a game which is changing very quickly but those few weeks in South Africa convinced me that there are some good young umpires coming through.

I would love to do some mentoring with the young English umpires as well. I've spoken to Chris Kelly about the possibility and it is something to consider for the future, but they need me on the field at the moment and that's where I will be in 2020. I'm looking forward to it. It will be my first full domestic season for 14 years and I expect mainly to be appointed to second division games in the County Championship so that the new group coming through can get as much experience as possible in Division One. It's going to be a busy summer, particularly the period during The Hundred in July and August, but as long as I am enjoying it I will carry on.

Jo is going to come with me on a few trips as well which will be nice, providing her satnav skills improve – although I don't think we'll be driving around and parking up at grounds in a camper van like my old colleague Roy Palmer used to do! It will certainly be enjoyable to do a couple of games at Hove and be able to walk to work, just like I did 40-odd years earlier when I started playing for Sussex.

I owe the ECB a lot because when I was roaming around the world on the international circuit they always looked after me, and found me as many games as I needed when I was back in England and looking to keep my eye in. I could theoretically carry on for another three years until I'm 65, but I will probably reassess at the end of 2020, or even during the season. As long as I'm enjoying myself, I will carry on, but they are long days and I ain't getting any younger. At least I will start the 2020 English season with a couple of local games. My first two games are both at Hove!

Will I ever stand in an international fixture again? Yes, I can see myself doing a women's international at Hove, a Lions game or an under-19 Test somewhere but it will be in this country, not overseas. The South Africa experience gave me a taste for mentoring umpires but my days standing in international matches are over. It's been a privilege and I wouldn't have changed any of it.

Bibliography

Pringle, Derek: *Pushing the Boundaries: Cricket in the Eighties* (Hodder & Stoughton, 2018).

Ramprakash, Mark: *Strictly Me: My Life under the Spotlight* (Mainstream Publishing, 2009).

Talbot, Bruce: *Sussex CCC Match of My Life* (Pitch Publishing, 2012).

Talbot, Bruce & Weaver, Paul: *The Longest Journey* (Sutton Publishing, 2004).

Wisden Almanack (John Wisden, various).

Websites consulted: *Cricinfo, Cricket Archive*